50 French Pastry Artistry Recipes for Home

By: Kelly Johnson

Table of Contents

- Classic Croissants
- Chocolate Eclairs with Vanilla Pastry Cream
- Raspberry Almond Tart
- Paris-Brest
- Lemon Madeleines
- Opera Cake
- Tarte Tatin
- Millefeuille (Napoleon)
- Pain Perdu (French Toast)
- Pâte à Choux Swans
- Gateau Saint-Honoré
- Chocolate Mousse
- Financiers
- Cherry Clafoutis
- Gougères (Cheese Puffs)
- Canelés de Bordeaux
- Palmiers (Elephant Ears)
- Raspberry and Pistachio Tartlets
- Buche de Noël (Yule Log)
- Strawberry Charlotte
- Profiteroles with Salted Caramel Sauce
- Crème Brûlée
- Kouign-Amann
- Cherry Pistachio Galette
- Brioche aux Pralines
- Pain d'Épices (Spice Bread)
- Macarons
- Pissaladière
- Flan Parisien
- Almond Croissants
- Tarte au Citron (Lemon Tart)
- Pâte Sablée Tart Shells
- Chausson aux Pommes (Apple Turnovers)
- Dark Chocolate Tarte Tatin
- Raspberry Rose Choux au Craquelin

- Pineapple Coconut Opera Cake
- Lemon Verbena Madeleines
- Strawberry Rhubarb Tart
- Gateau Basque
- Raspberry Pistachio Financiers
- Chocolatine (Pain au Chocolat)
- Pear Frangipane Tart
- Tiramisu Eclairs
- Apricot Pistachio Galette
- Matcha Green Tea Madeleines
- Peach Melba Millefeuille
- Blueberry Lavender Macarons
- Orange Blossom Madeleine Tartlets
- Hazelnut Dacquoise
- Prune Armagnac Clafoutis

Classic Croissants

Ingredients:

For the Dough:

- 4 cups all-purpose flour
- 1/4 cup granulated sugar
- 1 tablespoon active dry yeast
- 1 1/4 cups cold whole milk
- 1/4 cup cold water
- 1 tablespoon salt
- 1 1/4 cups unsalted butter, cold

For the Butter Block:

- 1 1/4 cups unsalted butter, cold

Instructions:

Prepare the Dough:

In a small bowl, combine the cold milk and water. Dissolve the yeast and sugar in the mixture. Let it sit for about 5 minutes until frothy.
In a large mixing bowl, combine the flour and salt. Add the yeast mixture and mix until just combined.
Knead the dough on a lightly floured surface for about 5 minutes. Form it into a rectangle, wrap it in plastic wrap, and refrigerate for 1 hour.

Prepare the Butter Block:

Place the cold butter between two sheets of parchment paper. Using a rolling pin, pound the butter to flatten it into a rectangle.
Refrigerate the butter while the dough is chilling.

Create the Laminated Dough:

Roll out the chilled dough on a floured surface into a larger rectangle.
Place the butter block in the center of the dough and fold the dough over it like a letter.

Roll out the dough again, fold it into thirds, and refrigerate for 30 minutes. Repeat this process three more times.

Shape and Proof the Croissants:

After the final fold, refrigerate the dough for at least 1 hour or overnight.
Roll out the chilled dough into a large rectangle and cut it into triangles.
Roll each triangle tightly from the wider end to the tip, creating the classic croissant shape.
Place the shaped croissants on a baking sheet lined with parchment paper.
Allow the croissants to proof at room temperature for 2-3 hours or until they double in size.

Bake the Croissants:

Preheat the oven to 400°F (200°C).
Brush the proofed croissants with an egg wash for a shiny finish.
Bake for 15-20 minutes or until the croissants are golden brown and flaky.
Allow the croissants to cool slightly before serving.

Tips:

- Ensure that the butter and dough remain cold throughout the process to achieve the flaky layers.
- Experiment with fillings like chocolate or almond paste for variations.

Making classic croissants requires patience and precision, but the result is a batch of delicious, homemade pastries that are well worth the effort. Enjoy the process and the delightful aroma that fills your kitchen!

Chocolate Eclairs with Vanilla Pastry Cream

Ingredients:

For the Choux Pastry:

- 1 cup water
- 1/2 cup unsalted butter
- 1 cup all-purpose flour
- 4 large eggs

For the Vanilla Pastry Cream:

- 2 cups whole milk
- 1/2 cup granulated sugar
- 4 large egg yolks
- 1/4 cup cornstarch
- 1 teaspoon vanilla extract

For the Chocolate Ganache:

- 6 ounces semisweet chocolate, chopped
- 1/2 cup heavy cream
- 2 tablespoons unsalted butter

Instructions:

Prepare the Choux Pastry:

Preheat the oven to 425°F (220°C). Line a baking sheet with parchment paper.
In a saucepan, combine water and butter over medium heat. Bring to a boil.
Add flour all at once and stir vigorously with a wooden spoon until the mixture forms a ball. Remove from heat.
Let the dough cool for a couple of minutes. Add eggs one at a time, beating well after each addition. The dough should be smooth and shiny.
Transfer the dough to a piping bag fitted with a large round tip. Pipe 4-inch lengths onto the prepared baking sheet.
Bake for 15 minutes at 425°F (220°C), then reduce the temperature to 375°F (190°C) and bake for an additional 15-20 minutes or until golden brown and puffed.
Allow the eclairs to cool completely on a wire rack.

Prepare the Vanilla Pastry Cream:

In a saucepan, heat the milk until it just starts to simmer.
In a bowl, whisk together sugar, egg yolks, and cornstarch until well combined.
Gradually pour the hot milk into the egg mixture, whisking constantly.
Return the mixture to the saucepan and cook over medium heat, whisking continuously until it thickens.
Remove from heat, stir in vanilla extract, and transfer the pastry cream to a bowl. Cover with plastic wrap, ensuring it touches the surface of the cream to prevent a skin from forming.
Refrigerate the pastry cream until chilled.

Prepare the Chocolate Ganache:

Place chopped chocolate in a heatproof bowl.
In a small saucepan, heat the heavy cream until it just starts to simmer. Pour it over the chopped chocolate.
Let it sit for a minute, then stir until smooth. Add butter and stir until well combined.

Assemble the Eclairs:

Slice the cooled eclairs horizontally.
Fill each eclair with vanilla pastry cream using a piping bag.
Dip the top of each filled eclair into the chocolate ganache.
Allow the chocolate to set before serving.

Tips:

- Be patient while making the pastry cream, ensuring it thickens properly to achieve a smooth texture.
- You can customize the filling with different flavors like coffee, chocolate, or hazelnut.

Enjoy these homemade chocolate eclairs with vanilla pastry cream – a perfect blend of light choux pastry, creamy filling, and rich chocolate ganache!

Raspberry Almond Tart

Ingredients:

For the Tart Crust:

- 1 1/4 cups all-purpose flour
- 1/2 cup unsalted butter, cold and cut into small cubes
- 1/4 cup granulated sugar
- 1/4 teaspoon salt
- 1 large egg yolk
- 1-2 tablespoons cold water

For the Almond Filling:

- 1 cup almond flour
- 1/2 cup granulated sugar
- 1/4 cup unsalted butter, softened
- 1 teaspoon almond extract
- 1 large egg

For the Raspberry Topping:

- 2 cups fresh raspberries
- 2 tablespoons raspberry jam or preserves

Instructions:

1. Make the Tart Crust:

a. In a food processor, combine the flour, sugar, and salt.

b. Add the cold, cubed butter and pulse until the mixture resembles coarse crumbs.

c. In a small bowl, whisk together the egg yolk and 1 tablespoon of cold water.

d. Add the egg yolk mixture to the flour mixture and pulse until the dough comes together. If needed, add an additional tablespoon of water.

e. Turn the dough out onto a lightly floured surface, knead it briefly, and then shape it into a disk. Wrap it in plastic wrap and refrigerate for at least 30 minutes.

2. Preheat the Oven:

Preheat your oven to 375°F (190°C).

3. Roll Out the Dough:

Roll out the chilled dough on a floured surface to fit your tart pan. Press the dough into the tart pan, trimming any excess.

4. Make the Almond Filling:

a. In a bowl, mix together almond flour, sugar, softened butter, almond extract, and egg until well combined.

b. Spread the almond filling evenly over the tart crust.

5. Bake the Tart:

Bake the tart in the preheated oven for about 20-25 minutes, or until the crust is golden and the almond filling is set.

6. Prepare the Raspberry Topping:

While the tart is baking, gently heat the raspberry jam in a small saucepan until it becomes liquid.

7. Assemble the Tart:

Once the tart is out of the oven, let it cool slightly. Arrange fresh raspberries on top of the almond filling, and then brush the raspberries with the melted raspberry jam for a shiny glaze.

8. Serve:

Allow the tart to cool completely before slicing and serving. You can also dust it with powdered sugar for an extra touch.

Enjoy your delicious Raspberry Almond Tart!

Paris-Brest

Ingredients:

For the Choux Pastry:

- 1/2 cup water
- 1/2 cup whole milk
- 1/2 cup unsalted butter, cut into small pieces
- 1/4 teaspoon salt
- 1 cup all-purpose flour
- 4 large eggs

For the Praline Cream:

- 1 1/4 cups whole milk
- 1/3 cup granulated sugar
- 3 large egg yolks
- 2 tablespoons cornstarch
- 1 teaspoon vanilla extract
- 1/2 cup hazelnuts, toasted and finely ground
- 1/2 cup powdered sugar (for dusting)

For the Praline Paste:

- 1 cup hazelnuts
- 1/2 cup granulated sugar

For Garnish:

- Sliced almonds (optional)

Instructions:

1. Make the Praline Paste:

a. Preheat the oven to 350°F (175°C).

b. Toast the hazelnuts on a baking sheet for about 10-12 minutes, or until fragrant.

c. In a saucepan, caramelize the sugar until it turns amber in color.

d. Add the toasted hazelnuts to the caramelized sugar, stirring quickly to coat the nuts.

e. Transfer the mixture to a parchment-lined tray, let it cool, and then break it into pieces.

f. Grind the caramelized hazelnuts in a food processor until you get a smooth paste. This is your praline paste.

2. Make the Choux Pastry:

a. Preheat your oven to 400°F (200°C) and line a baking sheet with parchment paper.

b. In a saucepan, combine water, milk, butter, and salt. Bring to a boil.

c. Add the flour all at once, stirring vigorously with a wooden spoon until the mixture forms a ball and pulls away from the sides of the pan.

d. Remove from heat and let it cool for a couple of minutes.

e. Add the eggs one at a time, beating well after each addition until the dough is smooth.

f. Transfer the choux pastry to a piping bag fitted with a large round tip.

3. Form the Paris-Brest:

a. Pipe a large ring of choux pastry onto the prepared baking sheet. You can use a round template to guide you.

b. Bake in the preheated oven for 35-40 minutes or until the pastry is golden brown and puffed. Let it cool completely.

4. Make the Praline Cream:

a. In a saucepan, heat the milk until it just begins to simmer.

b. In a bowl, whisk together the sugar, egg yolks, cornstarch, and vanilla extract.

c. Gradually pour the hot milk into the egg mixture, whisking constantly.

d. Return the mixture to the saucepan and cook over medium heat, stirring constantly, until it thickens.

e. Remove from heat and stir in the hazelnut praline paste. Let the cream cool completely.

5. Assemble the Paris-Brest:

a. Once the choux pastry is cooled, carefully slice it in half horizontally.

b. Pipe or spoon the praline cream onto the bottom half of the pastry.

c. Place the top half of the pastry back on the cream, gently pressing down.

6. Garnish and Serve:

a. Dust the Paris-Brest with powdered sugar and garnish with sliced almonds if desired.

b. Slice and serve the Paris-Brest. It's best enjoyed fresh.

This alternative Paris-Brest recipe offers the same delightful combination of choux pastry and praline cream with a slight twist in the praline paste. Enjoy the rich and nutty flavors of this classic French pastry!

Lemon Madeleines

Ingredients:

For the Madeleines:

- 2/3 cup all-purpose flour
- 1/2 teaspoon baking powder
- 1/4 teaspoon salt
- Zest of 2 lemons
- 1/2 cup unsalted butter, melted and cooled
- 2 large eggs
- 1/2 cup granulated sugar
- 1 teaspoon vanilla extract

For the Glaze (optional):

- 1 cup powdered sugar
- 2-3 tablespoons fresh lemon juice

Instructions:

1. Preheat the Oven:

Preheat your oven to 375°F (190°C). Grease and flour your Madeleine molds.

2. Make the Madeleine Batter:

a. In a bowl, whisk together the flour, baking powder, and salt. Add the lemon zest and mix well.

b. In another bowl, beat the eggs and sugar together until light and fluffy.

c. Gradually add the melted butter and vanilla extract to the egg mixture, stirring continuously.

d. Gently fold the dry ingredients into the wet ingredients until just combined. Be careful not to overmix.

3. Chill the Batter:

Cover the bowl with plastic wrap and refrigerate the batter for at least 30 minutes. This helps the Madeleines achieve their characteristic hump.

4. Fill the Madeleine Molds:

Spoon the chilled batter into the prepared Madeleine molds, filling each mold about 3/4 full.

5. Bake:

Bake in the preheated oven for about 10-12 minutes or until the edges are golden brown and the tops spring back when lightly touched.

6. Make the Glaze (Optional):

While the Madeleines are baking, prepare the glaze by whisking together powdered sugar and fresh lemon juice until smooth.

7. Cool and Glaze:

a. Allow the Madeleines to cool in the molds for a couple of minutes.

b. Remove them from the molds and transfer to a wire rack to cool completely.

c. If desired, dip the cooled Madeleines into the glaze or drizzle the glaze over the top.

8. Serve:

Once the glaze has set, serve the Lemon Madeleines with a cup of tea or coffee. Enjoy their delicate texture and bright citrus flavor!

These Lemon Madeleines are perfect for any occasion, and their unique shape and citrusy goodness make them a lovely addition to your dessert repertoire.

Opera Cake

Ingredients:

For the Almond Sponge Cake (Joconde):

- 1 cup almond flour
- 1 cup powdered sugar
- 3 large eggs
- 3 large egg whites
- 1/4 cup granulated sugar
- 1/2 cup all-purpose flour
- 2 tablespoons unsalted butter, melted

For the Coffee Buttercream:

- 1 cup unsalted butter, softened
- 1 cup powdered sugar
- 2 tablespoons instant coffee granules, dissolved in 2 tablespoons hot water
- 1 teaspoon vanilla extract

For the Chocolate Ganache:

- 4 ounces dark chocolate, finely chopped
- 1/2 cup heavy cream

For the Chocolate Glaze:

- 4 ounces dark chocolate, finely chopped
- 1/3 cup heavy cream
- 1 tablespoon unsalted butter

Instructions:

1. Make the Almond Sponge Cake (Joconde):

a. Preheat your oven to 425°F (220°C). Grease and line a baking sheet with parchment paper.

b. In a bowl, sift together almond flour and powdered sugar.

c. In a separate bowl, beat the eggs until pale and fluffy.

d. In another bowl, whip the egg whites until soft peaks form. Gradually add granulated sugar and continue whipping until stiff peaks form.

e. Gently fold the beaten eggs into the almond flour mixture.

f. In a small bowl, mix a portion of this batter with melted butter and then fold it back into the main batter.

g. Sift in the all-purpose flour and fold until just combined.

h. Spread the batter evenly onto the prepared baking sheet and bake for about 7-10 minutes or until the cake is set and lightly golden.

i. Let the cake cool completely before trimming it to fit your desired cake shape.

2. Make the Coffee Buttercream:

a. Dissolve instant coffee granules in hot water and let it cool.

b. In a bowl, beat softened butter until creamy.

c. Gradually add powdered sugar and beat until smooth.

d. Add the cooled coffee mixture and vanilla extract. Beat until well combined.

3. Assemble the Opera Cake:

a. Place one layer of the almond sponge cake on a serving platter.

b. Spread a layer of coffee buttercream over the cake.

c. Continue layering the remaining almond sponge cake and coffee buttercream, finishing with a layer of buttercream on top.

4. Make the Chocolate Ganache:

a. Place finely chopped dark chocolate in a heatproof bowl.

b. Heat the heavy cream in a small saucepan until it just begins to boil.

c. Pour the hot cream over the chopped chocolate and let it sit for a minute.

d. Stir until the chocolate is melted and the ganache is smooth.

e. Allow the ganache to cool slightly, then pour it over the assembled cake, spreading it evenly with a spatula.

5. Make the Chocolate Glaze:

a. Place finely chopped dark chocolate in a heatproof bowl.

b. Heat the heavy cream and butter in a small saucepan until it just begins to boil.

c. Pour the hot cream mixture over the chopped chocolate and let it sit for a minute.

d. Stir until the chocolate is melted and the glaze is smooth.

6. Finish the Opera Cake:

a. Pour the chocolate glaze over the set ganache layer, ensuring it covers the entire surface.

b. Allow the glaze to set at room temperature or in the refrigerator.

7. Serve:

Once the glaze is set, slice and serve the Opera Cake. Enjoy the layers of almond sponge, coffee buttercream, and rich chocolate!

The Opera Cake is a masterpiece of textures and flavors, making it a showstopper for special occasions.

Tarte Tatin

Ingredients:

For the Tarte Tatin:

- 6-8 medium-sized apples (preferably tart varieties like Granny Smith), peeled, cored, and halved
- 1 cup granulated sugar
- 1/2 cup unsalted butter
- 1 tablespoon lemon juice
- 1 teaspoon vanilla extract
- Pinch of salt
- 1 package of puff pastry (store-bought or homemade)

For Serving (Optional):

- Whipped cream or vanilla ice cream

Instructions:

1. Preheat the Oven:

Preheat your oven to 375°F (190°C).

2. Caramelize the Apples:

a. In a 10- or 12-inch ovenproof skillet or Tatin dish, melt the butter over medium heat.

b. Add sugar and cook, stirring occasionally, until the sugar dissolves and turns into a golden caramel.

c. Remove the skillet from heat and carefully arrange the apple halves, cut side down, in a circular pattern on top of the caramel.

d. Sprinkle the apples with lemon juice, vanilla extract, and a pinch of salt.

3. Cook on the Stovetop:

a. Return the skillet to medium heat and cook the apples in the caramel for about 15-20 minutes or until they are slightly softened and the caramel has thickened.

4. Roll Out the Puff Pastry:

a. Roll out the puff pastry on a lightly floured surface to a size slightly larger than the diameter of the skillet.

5. Assemble the Tarte Tatin:

a. Carefully place the puff pastry over the caramelized apples, tucking in the edges around the apples.

b. Use a sharp knife to make a few small slits in the puff pastry to allow steam to escape during baking.

6. Bake:

a. Bake in the preheated oven for 20-25 minutes or until the puff pastry is golden brown and cooked through.

7. Invert and Serve:

a. Once out of the oven, let the Tarte Tatin cool for a couple of minutes.

b. Place a serving platter over the skillet and carefully invert the Tarte Tatin onto the platter. Be cautious, as the caramel will be hot.

c. Serve the Tarte Tatin warm, with a dollop of whipped cream or a scoop of vanilla ice cream if desired.

8. Enjoy:

Slice and serve the Tarte Tatin, ensuring that each serving includes a portion of the caramelized apples and the flaky puff pastry.

Tarte Tatin is a wonderful dessert that highlights the natural sweetness of caramelized apples with the buttery goodness of puff pastry. It's a perfect treat for any occasion, and the upside-down presentation adds a touch of elegance to your table.

Millefeuille (Napoleon)

Ingredients:

For the Puff Pastry:

- 1 sheet of store-bought puff pastry (or homemade if you prefer)
- Powdered sugar for dusting (optional)

For the Pastry Cream:

- 2 cups whole milk
- 1 vanilla bean or 1 teaspoon vanilla extract
- 6 large egg yolks
- 1/2 cup granulated sugar
- 1/3 cup cornstarch
- 2 tablespoons unsalted butter

For the Glaze:

- 1 cup powdered sugar
- 2-3 tablespoons water
- 1/2 teaspoon vanilla extract (optional)

Instructions:

1. Prepare the Puff Pastry:

a. Preheat your oven according to the puff pastry package instructions or to 400°F (200°C).

b. Roll out the puff pastry sheet on a lightly floured surface to your desired thickness.

c. Cut the puff pastry into three equal-sized rectangles.

d. Place the rectangles on a parchment-lined baking sheet and prick the surface with a fork to prevent excessive puffing.

e. Bake according to the package instructions or until the pastry is golden brown and puffed.

f. Let the puff pastry cool completely.

2. Make the Pastry Cream:

a. In a saucepan, heat the milk over medium heat. If using a vanilla bean, split it open, scrape the seeds, and add both the seeds and the pod to the milk. If using vanilla extract, add it later.

b. In a bowl, whisk together the egg yolks, sugar, and cornstarch until well combined.

c. Once the milk is hot (but not boiling), remove the vanilla pod if used, and gradually whisk it into the egg mixture.

d. Return the mixture to the saucepan and cook over medium heat, stirring constantly until it thickens into a smooth pastry cream.

e. Remove from heat, stir in the butter and vanilla extract (if using), and let the pastry cream cool completely. Cover it with plastic wrap directly on the surface to prevent a skin from forming.

3. Assemble the Millefeuille:

a. Place one puff pastry rectangle on a serving platter.

b. Spread a layer of pastry cream evenly over the first puff pastry layer.

c. Place the second puff pastry rectangle on top of the pastry cream, pressing down gently.

d. Add another layer of pastry cream.

e. Top with the third puff pastry rectangle.

f. Optionally, dust the top with powdered sugar for a decorative touch.

4. Make the Glaze:

a. In a bowl, whisk together powdered sugar, water, and vanilla extract (if using) until you achieve a smooth, pourable glaze.

5. Glaze the Millefeuille:

a. Pour the glaze over the top layer of the Millefeuille, allowing it to drizzle down the sides.

6. Chill and Serve:

a. Refrigerate the assembled Millefeuille for at least an hour to allow the layers to set.

b. Once chilled, slice and serve the Millefeuille.

Millefeuille is a decadent and visually stunning dessert, showcasing the delicate layers of puff pastry and luscious pastry cream. It's sure to impress your guests with its combination of textures and flavors.

Pain Perdu (French Toast)

Ingredients:

- 4 slices of bread (French or any other type you prefer)
- 2 large eggs
- 1/2 cup milk
- 2 tablespoons granulated sugar
- 1 teaspoon vanilla extract
- 1/4 teaspoon ground cinnamon (optional)
- Pinch of salt
- Butter or cooking oil for frying
- Maple syrup, powdered sugar, or fresh berries for serving (optional)

Instructions:

1. Prepare the Egg Mixture:

a. In a shallow dish, whisk together the eggs, milk, sugar, vanilla extract, ground cinnamon (if using), and a pinch of salt. Ensure that the ingredients are well combined.

2. Soak the Bread:

a. Place each slice of bread into the egg mixture, allowing it to soak for about 15-20 seconds on each side. Ensure that the bread is coated evenly but not overly saturated.

3. Heat the Pan:

a. Heat a skillet or griddle over medium heat. Add a small amount of butter or cooking oil to prevent sticking.

4. Cook the French Toast:

a. Place the soaked bread slices on the hot skillet and cook for 2-3 minutes on each side or until they turn golden brown and have a slightly crispy texture.

5. Repeat:

a. Repeat the process with the remaining slices of bread.

6. Serve:

a. Transfer the cooked Pain Perdu to a serving plate.

b. Serve hot, topped with maple syrup, powdered sugar, fresh berries, or any other toppings of your choice.

7. Enjoy:

a. Enjoy your homemade Pain Perdu as a delicious and comforting breakfast treat!

Tips:

- Use slightly stale bread for better absorption of the egg mixture.
- Customize the flavor by adding a dash of nutmeg or orange zest to the egg mixture.
- Serve with your favorite toppings, such as whipped cream, sliced bananas, or a dollop of yogurt.

Pain Perdu is a versatile dish that can be easily adapted to suit your taste preferences. It's a delightful way to start your day with a comforting and satisfying breakfast.

Pâte à Choux Swans

Ingredients:

For the Pâte à Choux:

- 1/2 cup (1 stick) unsalted butter
- 1 cup water
- 1/4 teaspoon salt
- 1 cup all-purpose flour
- 4 large eggs

For the Filling:

- Vanilla custard or whipped cream

For Assembly:

- Powdered sugar for dusting
- Chocolate ganache (optional)

Instructions:

1. Preheat the Oven:

Preheat your oven to 425°F (220°C). Line a baking sheet with parchment paper.

2. Make the Pâte à Choux:

a. In a medium-sized saucepan, combine the butter, water, and salt. Heat over medium heat until the butter is melted and the mixture comes to a boil.

b. Reduce the heat to low and add the flour all at once. Stir vigorously with a wooden spoon until the mixture forms a ball and pulls away from the sides of the pan. This is the Pâte à Choux dough.

c. Transfer the dough to a mixing bowl and let it cool for a few minutes.

d. Add the eggs one at a time, beating well after each addition. Make sure each egg is fully incorporated before adding the next. The dough should become smooth and glossy.

e. Transfer the Pâte à Choux dough to a piping bag fitted with a large round tip.

3. Pipe the Swans:

a. On the prepared baking sheet, pipe an "S" shape for the swan neck and body. For the head, pipe a small round shape at the top of the "S."

b. Wet your finger and gently smooth any peaks or imperfections in the dough.

4. Bake:

a. Bake in the preheated oven for 15 minutes.

b. Reduce the oven temperature to 375°F (190°C) and continue baking for an additional 10-15 minutes or until the swans are golden brown and puffed.

c. Remove from the oven and let them cool completely on a wire rack.

5. Fill the Swans:

a. Once the swans are cool, cut the tops off horizontally.

b. Fill the bottom part with vanilla custard or whipped cream.

c. Place the top part back on the filled swan.

6. Assembly:

a. Dust the filled swans with powdered sugar.

b. Optionally, drizzle with chocolate ganache for added decadence.

7. Serve:

Arrange your Pâte à Choux swans on a serving platter and serve them as a charming and delicious dessert.

Pâte à Choux swans make for an impressive presentation, perfect for special occasions or elegant dessert tables. Enjoy the delicate, crisp pastry filled with creamy goodness!

Gateau Saint-Honoré

Ingredients:

For the Puff Pastry:

- 1 sheet of puff pastry (store-bought or homemade)

For the Choux Pastry:

- 1/2 cup water
- 1/2 cup whole milk
- 1/2 cup unsalted butter
- 1/4 teaspoon salt
- 1 cup all-purpose flour
- 4 large eggs

For the Chiboust Cream:

- 1 cup whole milk
- 1 vanilla bean or 1 teaspoon vanilla extract
- 4 large egg yolks
- 1/2 cup granulated sugar
- 2 tablespoons cornstarch
- 1/2 cup unsalted butter, softened
- 1/2 cup Italian meringue (made with egg whites and sugar)

For Assembly:

- Caramelized sugar for decoration
- Whipped cream (optional)
- Fresh berries for garnish (optional)

Instructions:

1. Prepare the Puff Pastry:

a. Preheat your oven according to the puff pastry package instructions or to 400°F (200°C).

b. Roll out the puff pastry sheet on a lightly floured surface to your desired thickness.

c. Cut the puff pastry into a circle, about 9 inches in diameter.

d. Place the puff pastry circle on a parchment-lined baking sheet and bake according to the package instructions or until it's golden brown and puffed.

e. Let the puff pastry cool completely.

2. Make the Choux Pastry:

a. Preheat your oven to 400°F (200°C).

b. In a saucepan, combine water, milk, butter, and salt. Bring to a boil.

c. Add the flour all at once, stirring vigorously with a wooden spoon until the mixture forms a ball and pulls away from the sides of the pan.

d. Remove from heat and let it cool for a couple of minutes.

e. Add the eggs one at a time, beating well after each addition until the dough is smooth.

f. Transfer the choux pastry to a piping bag fitted with a large round tip.

g. Pipe a ring of choux pastry around the edge of the cooled puff pastry circle.

3. Bake the Choux Pastry:

a. Bake in the preheated oven for 30-35 minutes or until the choux pastry is golden brown and puffed.

b. Let it cool completely.

4. Make the Chiboust Cream:

a. In a saucepan, heat the milk over medium heat. If using a vanilla bean, split it open, scrape the seeds, and add both the seeds and the pod to the milk. If using vanilla extract, add it later.

b. In a bowl, whisk together the egg yolks, sugar, and cornstarch until well combined.

c. Once the milk is hot (but not boiling), remove the vanilla pod if used, and gradually whisk it into the egg mixture.

d. Return the mixture to the saucepan and cook over medium heat, stirring constantly until it thickens into a smooth pastry cream.

e. Remove from heat, transfer to a bowl, and let it cool completely.

f. Once cooled, fold in the softened butter and then gently fold in the Italian meringue.

5. Fill the Gateau Saint-Honoré:

a. Spoon the Chiboust cream into the center of the baked puff pastry and spread it evenly within the ring of choux pastry.

6. Caramelize Sugar:

a. Caramelize sugar by heating it in a saucepan until it turns amber in color. Drizzle the caramelized sugar over the Chiboust cream in a decorative pattern.

7. Optional Garnish:

a. Optionally, garnish with whipped cream and fresh berries.

8. Serve:

a. Slice and serve your Gateau Saint-Honoré, showcasing the layers of puff pastry, choux pastry, and luscious Chiboust cream.

Gateau Saint-Honoré is a show-stopping dessert that requires some effort but is well worth it for special occasions or celebrations. It's a beautiful and delicious tribute to French pastry craftsmanship.

Chocolate Mousse

Ingredients:

- 7 ounces (200g) good-quality dark chocolate, finely chopped
- 3.5 ounces (100g) unsalted butter, cut into small pieces
- 3 large eggs, separated
- 1/4 cup (50g) granulated sugar
- 1 teaspoon pure vanilla extract
- A pinch of salt
- 1 cup (240ml) heavy cream
- Additional whipped cream and chocolate shavings for garnish (optional)

Instructions:

1. Melt the Chocolate and Butter:

a. In a heatproof bowl, melt the chopped chocolate and butter together. You can do this by placing the bowl over a pot of simmering water (double boiler) or by using short bursts in the microwave, stirring in between until smooth.

b. Once melted, remove the bowl from the heat and let it cool slightly.

2. Add Egg Yolks and Sugar:

a. In a separate bowl, whisk together the egg yolks, sugar, vanilla extract, and a pinch of salt until the mixture becomes pale and slightly thick.

b. Gradually add the melted chocolate mixture to the egg yolk mixture, stirring continuously until well combined.

3. Whip the Egg Whites:

a. In a clean, dry bowl, whip the egg whites until stiff peaks form.

4. Fold in the Egg Whites:

a. Gently fold the whipped egg whites into the chocolate mixture in two or three additions. Be careful not to deflate the egg whites, and make sure there are no white streaks remaining.

5. Whip the Heavy Cream:

a. In another bowl, whip the heavy cream until soft peaks form.

6. Fold in the Whipped Cream:

a. Gently fold the whipped cream into the chocolate mixture until smooth and well combined.

7. Chill:

a. Spoon or pipe the chocolate mousse into serving glasses or bowls.

b. Refrigerate the mousse for at least 2-3 hours, or until set.

8. Garnish and Serve:

a. Before serving, you can garnish the chocolate mousse with additional whipped cream and chocolate shavings if desired.

9. Enjoy:

Serve the chocolate mousse chilled and enjoy its rich and creamy texture!

This classic chocolate mousse recipe yields a decadent and velvety dessert. It's perfect for special occasions or when you're craving a luxurious chocolate treat. Feel free to adjust the sweetness or experiment with different types of chocolate for variations.

Financiers

Ingredients:

- 1 cup (225g) unsalted butter
- 1 cup (100g) almond flour
- 1 1/2 cups (180g) powdered sugar
- 1/2 cup (60g) all-purpose flour
- 1/2 teaspoon salt
- 6 large egg whites
- 1 teaspoon vanilla extract
- Optional: Sliced almonds or whole almonds for garnish

Instructions:

1. Preheat the Oven:

Preheat your oven to 375°F (190°C). Grease and flour your financier molds or mini muffin tins.

2. Brown the Butter:

In a saucepan, melt the butter over medium heat. Continue to cook, swirling the pan occasionally until the butter turns a golden brown color and has a nutty aroma. Be careful not to let it burn. Remove from heat and let it cool slightly.

3. Mix Dry Ingredients:

In a mixing bowl, whisk together almond flour, powdered sugar, all-purpose flour, and salt.

4. Add Egg Whites:

In a separate bowl, whisk the egg whites until frothy but not stiff. Gradually fold the egg whites into the dry ingredients until well combined.

5. Add Browned Butter:

Pour the slightly cooled browned butter into the batter and stir until smooth and fully incorporated. Add vanilla extract and mix well.

6. Fill the Molds:

Fill the financier molds or mini muffin tins about 2/3 full with the batter.

7. Bake:

Bake in the preheated oven for about 12-15 minutes or until the financiers are golden brown around the edges and a toothpick inserted into the center comes out clean.

8. Cool:

Allow the financiers to cool in the molds for a few minutes before transferring them to a wire rack to cool completely.

9. Optional Garnish:

If desired, you can garnish the tops of the financiers with sliced almonds or whole almonds before baking.

10. Serve:

Once cooled, serve the financiers and enjoy these delicious, bite-sized almond cakes!

Financiers are a delightful treat that pairs well with coffee or tea. Their rich almond flavor and buttery texture make them a favorite for dessert or a sweet snack. You can also customize them by adding ingredients like chocolate chips or fruit pieces to the batter.

Cherry Clafoutis

Ingredients:

- 1 pound (about 450g) fresh cherries, pitted
- 1 cup (240ml) whole milk
- 3 large eggs
- 1/2 cup (100g) granulated sugar
- 1 teaspoon vanilla extract
- 1/2 cup (65g) all-purpose flour
- 1/4 teaspoon salt
- Butter for greasing the baking dish
- Powdered sugar for dusting (optional)

Instructions:

1. Preheat the Oven:

Preheat your oven to 350°F (175°C). Butter a baking dish (approximately 9 inches in diameter).

2. Prepare the Cherries:

a. Wash and pit the cherries. You can leave the pits in for a more traditional clafoutis flavor or remove them for easier eating.

3. Make the Batter:

a. In a blender or with a hand whisk, combine the milk, eggs, sugar, vanilla extract, flour, and salt. Blend or whisk until the batter is smooth and well combined.

4. Arrange the Cherries:

a. Place the pitted cherries in a single layer in the buttered baking dish.

5. Pour the Batter:

a. Pour the batter over the cherries in the baking dish. The batter will partially cover the cherries.

6. Bake:

a. Bake in the preheated oven for 40-45 minutes or until the clafoutis is set and golden brown on top. A toothpick inserted into the center should come out clean.

7. Cool:

a. Allow the Cherry Clafoutis to cool for a few minutes before serving. It will deflate slightly as it cools.

8. Dust with Powdered Sugar (Optional):

a. Just before serving, dust the top of the clafoutis with powdered sugar for a decorative touch.

9. Serve:

a. Serve the Cherry Clafoutis warm, either on its own or with a dollop of whipped cream or a scoop of vanilla ice cream.

Cherry Clafoutis is a rustic and comforting dessert that captures the sweetness of fresh cherries. The custard-like batter surrounds the fruit, creating a delightful contrast in textures. It's a wonderful treat, especially when cherries are in season.

Gougères (Cheese Puffs)

Ingredients:

- 1 cup water
- 1/2 cup unsalted butter
- 1/2 teaspoon salt
- 1 cup all-purpose flour
- 4 large eggs
- 1 1/2 cups grated Gruyère or Emmental cheese (or a combination)
- 1/2 teaspoon black pepper (optional)
- Pinch of nutmeg (optional)

Instructions:

1. Preheat the Oven:

Preheat your oven to 425°F (220°C). Line baking sheets with parchment paper.

2. Make the Choux Pastry:

a. In a medium saucepan, combine water, butter, and salt. Bring to a boil over medium heat.

b. Reduce heat to low and add the flour all at once. Stir vigorously with a wooden spoon until the mixture forms a ball and pulls away from the sides of the pan.

c. Remove from heat and let it cool for a couple of minutes.

3. Add Eggs:

a. Add the eggs one at a time, beating well after each addition. Make sure each egg is fully incorporated before adding the next. The dough should become smooth and glossy.

4. Add Cheese and Seasonings:

a. Stir in the grated cheese and, if desired, black pepper and a pinch of nutmeg. Mix until the cheese is evenly distributed.

5. Pipe or Spoon onto Baking Sheets:

a. Transfer the choux pastry to a piping bag fitted with a large round tip or simply use two spoons to drop mounds of dough onto the prepared baking sheets. Leave some space between each puff.

6. Bake:

a. Bake in the preheated oven for 15-20 minutes or until the Gougères are golden brown and puffed. Optionally, you can reduce the temperature to 375°F (190°C) after the first 10 minutes of baking for even browning.

7. Cool and Serve:

a. Allow the Gougères to cool slightly before serving. They can be enjoyed warm or at room temperature.

8. Optional Variations:

a. For additional flavor, you can add herbs like thyme or rosemary to the dough.

b. Experiment with different cheeses to create unique flavor combinations.

9. Serve:

a. Arrange the Gougères on a platter and serve them as a delicious appetizer or snack.

Gougères are a delightful and versatile treat that combines the light and airy texture of choux pastry with the savory goodness of cheese. They're sure to be a hit at any gathering!

Canelés de Bordeaux

Ingredients:

- 2 cups whole milk
- 1 1/2 tablespoons unsalted butter
- 1 cup all-purpose flour
- 2 cups granulated sugar
- 1/2 teaspoon salt
- 4 large eggs
- 1 vanilla bean (or 1 teaspoon vanilla extract)
- 3 tablespoons dark rum

Instructions:

1. Prepare the Batter:

a. In a saucepan, heat the milk and butter until the butter is melted. Allow it to cool to lukewarm.

b. In a large mixing bowl, whisk together the flour, sugar, and salt.

c. Add the eggs one at a time, whisking well after each addition.

d. Pour in the lukewarm milk and butter mixture, and whisk until the batter is smooth and well combined.

e. Split the vanilla bean, scrape out the seeds, and add both the seeds and the pod to the batter. If using vanilla extract, add it later.

f. Stir in the rum and mix until the batter is homogenous.

2. Rest the Batter:

a. Cover the bowl and let the batter rest in the refrigerator for at least 24 hours. This allows the flavors to develop.

3. Preheat the Oven and Prepare Molds:

a. Preheat your oven to 475°F (245°C).

b. Butter and flour your canelé molds thoroughly to ensure easy removal after baking.

4. Fill the Molds:

a. Pour the rested batter into the prepared canelé molds, filling them almost to the top.

5. Bake:

a. Place the molds in the preheated oven and bake at 475°F (245°C) for 15 minutes.

b. Reduce the temperature to 375°F (190°C) and continue baking for an additional 45 minutes or until the canelés have a dark, caramelized crust.

6. Cool and Demold:

a. Allow the canelés to cool in the molds for a few minutes before transferring them to a wire rack to cool completely.

b. Gently tap the molds to release the canelés.

7. Serve:

a. Serve the Canelés de Bordeaux at room temperature. They are best enjoyed within a day or two of baking.

Canelés de Bordeaux are a delightful blend of textures and flavors. The crispy caramelized exterior gives way to a soft, custardy center with hints of vanilla and rum. Enjoy these delicious pastries with a cup of coffee or tea for a true French treat.

Palmiers (Elephant Ears)

Ingredients:

- 1 sheet of puff pastry (store-bought or homemade)
- 1 cup granulated sugar (for sprinkling)

Instructions:

1. Preheat the Oven:

Preheat your oven to 400°F (200°C). Line a baking sheet with parchment paper.

2. Roll Out the Puff Pastry:

a. If using store-bought puff pastry, roll it out on a lightly floured surface to smooth out any seams.

b. If using homemade puff pastry, ensure it is rolled out to a rectangular shape.

3. Sprinkle with Sugar:

a. Sprinkle a generous layer of granulated sugar evenly over the entire surface of the puff pastry.

4. Fold the Edges:

a. Starting from one long edge, fold each side of the puff pastry toward the center, meeting in the middle. Ensure that the folds are even.

5. Fold Again:

a. Fold the pastry in half along the centerline, creating a double fold with sugar inside.

6. Slice into Palmiers:

a. Using a sharp knife, slice the folded puff pastry into 1/2-inch to 3/4-inch slices. You should see the layers of pastry and sugar.

7. Arrange on Baking Sheet:

a. Place the sliced Palmiers on the prepared baking sheet, leaving some space between each.

8. Bake:

a. Bake in the preheated oven for 12-15 minutes or until the Palmiers are golden brown and have caramelized edges.

9. Cool and Serve:

a. Allow the Palmiers to cool on the baking sheet for a few minutes before transferring them to a wire rack to cool completely.

10. Enjoy:

a. Serve the Palmiers as a delightful treat with your favorite hot beverage.

Palmiers are a simple yet elegant pastry that's perfect for snacking or as a sweet accompaniment to tea or coffee. Their impressive appearance and deliciously caramelized layers make them a popular choice for various occasions.

Raspberry and Pistachio Tartlets

Ingredients:

For the Tart Crust:

- 1 1/4 cups all-purpose flour
- 1/2 cup unsalted butter, cold and diced
- 1/4 cup granulated sugar
- 1/4 teaspoon salt
- 1 large egg yolk
- 2 tablespoons ice water

For the Pistachio Frangipane:

- 1/2 cup shelled pistachios, finely ground
- 1/3 cup granulated sugar
- 1/4 cup unsalted butter, softened
- 1 large egg
- 1 tablespoon all-purpose flour
- 1/2 teaspoon vanilla extract

For Assembly:

- Fresh raspberries
- Apricot jam or glaze for brushing (optional)
- Chopped pistachios for garnish (optional)
- Powdered sugar for dusting (optional)

Instructions:

1. Make the Tart Crust:

a. In a food processor, pulse together the flour, sugar, and salt.

b. Add the cold, diced butter and pulse until the mixture resembles coarse crumbs.

c. In a small bowl, whisk together the egg yolk and ice water. Add this mixture to the food processor and pulse until the dough just comes together.

d. Turn the dough out onto a floured surface, knead it slightly to bring it together, then shape it into a disk. Wrap it in plastic wrap and refrigerate for at least 30 minutes.

2. Prepare Pistachio Frangipane:

a. In a bowl, mix together the finely ground pistachios, sugar, softened butter, egg, flour, and vanilla extract until well combined.

3. Preheat the Oven:

a. Preheat your oven to 375°F (190°C).

4. Roll Out the Dough:

a. On a floured surface, roll out the chilled tart dough to about 1/8 inch thickness. Cut out small circles or squares to fit your tartlet molds.

5. Line Tartlet Molds:

a. Press the dough circles or squares into your tartlet molds, ensuring the dough is evenly distributed and there are no air bubbles.

6. Fill with Pistachio Frangipane:

a. Fill each tartlet mold with a spoonful of the prepared pistachio frangipane, spreading it evenly.

7. Bake:

a. Bake in the preheated oven for about 12-15 minutes or until the crust is golden brown and the frangipane is set.

8. Assembly:

a. Once the tartlets have cooled, arrange fresh raspberries on top. Optionally, brush the raspberries with apricot jam or glaze for a shiny finish.

b. Garnish with chopped pistachios and dust with powdered sugar if desired.

9. Serve:

a. Serve the Raspberry and Pistachio Tartlets at room temperature and enjoy!

These tartlets are not only visually appealing but also a delightful combination of textures and flavors. The buttery crust, nutty pistachio frangipane, and fresh raspberries create a perfect balance. They make for an elegant dessert or a sweet treat for any occasion.

Buche de Noël (Yule Log)

Ingredients:

For the Sponge Cake:

- 4 large eggs
- 3/4 cup granulated sugar
- 1 teaspoon vanilla extract
- 1/2 cup all-purpose flour
- 1/4 cup cocoa powder
- 1/4 teaspoon salt
- Powdered sugar for dusting

For the Buttercream:

- 1 cup unsalted butter, softened
- 2 cups powdered sugar
- 1 teaspoon vanilla extract
- 3 tablespoons cocoa powder (for chocolate buttercream)

For Filling:

- Raspberry jam or other fruit preserves (optional)

For Decoration:

- Additional cocoa powder (for dusting)
- Meringue mushrooms or other festive decorations

Instructions:

1. Preheat the Oven:

a. Preheat your oven to 375°F (190°C).

b. Line a jelly roll pan (approximately 10x15 inches) with parchment paper.

2. Make the Sponge Cake:

a. In a large bowl, beat the eggs and granulated sugar together until light and fluffy.

b. Add the vanilla extract and mix well.

c. In a separate bowl, sift together the flour, cocoa powder, and salt.

d. Gently fold the dry ingredients into the egg mixture until just combined.

e. Pour the batter into the prepared jelly roll pan and spread it evenly.

3. Bake:

a. Bake in the preheated oven for about 10-12 minutes or until the cake is set and springs back when lightly touched.

4. Roll the Sponge Cake:

a. While the cake is still warm, dust the surface with powdered sugar.

b. Invert the cake onto a clean kitchen towel and gently peel off the parchment paper.

c. Roll the cake, along with the towel, starting from one of the shorter ends. Allow it to cool completely in the rolled position.

5. Make the Buttercream:

a. In a large bowl, beat the softened butter until creamy.

b. Gradually add the powdered sugar and continue beating until light and fluffy.

c. Add vanilla extract. For chocolate buttercream, add cocoa powder and mix until well combined.

6. Fill and Assemble:

a. Unroll the cooled sponge cake and spread a thin layer of buttercream over the surface.

b. If desired, spread a thin layer of raspberry jam or fruit preserves over the buttercream.

c. Roll the cake back up, this time without the towel. Place it seam side down on a serving platter.

7. Frost the Log:

a. Frost the rolled cake with the remaining buttercream, creating a log-like texture with a spatula.

b. Optionally, use a fork or knife to create bark-like patterns on the buttercream.

8. Decorate:

a. Dust the Bûche de Noël with additional cocoa powder to resemble dirt.

b. Decorate with meringue mushrooms or other festive decorations.

9. Chill and Serve:

a. Refrigerate the Bûche de Noël for at least a couple of hours before serving to set the buttercream.

b. Slice and serve chilled.

Bûche de Noël is a show-stopping dessert that adds a festive touch to your Christmas celebrations. Enjoy the rich, chocolaty flavors and the artful presentation reminiscent of a yule log.

Strawberry Charlotte

Ingredients:

For the Strawberry Mousse:

- 2 cups fresh strawberries, hulled and chopped
- 1/2 cup granulated sugar
- 2 tablespoons lemon juice
- 2 teaspoons gelatin powder
- 1/4 cup cold water
- 2 cups heavy cream

For the Ladyfinger Base:

- 24-30 ladyfinger biscuits (savoiardi)
- 1/2 cup strawberry jam or preserves
- 1/4 cup water (for brushing ladyfingers)

For Garnish (optional):

- Fresh strawberries
- Mint leaves
- Powdered sugar

Instructions:

1. Prepare the Strawberry Puree:

a. In a blender or food processor, blend the fresh strawberries until smooth.

b. Strain the strawberry puree to remove seeds, if desired.

c. Mix the strawberry puree with sugar and lemon juice in a saucepan. Heat over medium heat until the sugar dissolves. Allow it to cool.

2. Bloom the Gelatin:

a. In a small bowl, sprinkle gelatin over cold water. Let it sit for a few minutes until it blooms.

b. Microwave the bloomed gelatin for about 10 seconds or until it's fully dissolved. Allow it to cool slightly.

3. Make the Strawberry Mousse:

a. In a large bowl, whip the heavy cream until soft peaks form.

b. Gently fold the strawberry puree mixture into the whipped cream until well combined.

c. Gradually add the dissolved gelatin and continue folding until the mousse is smooth.

4. Prepare the Ladyfinger Base:

a. Line the sides of a round springform pan with parchment paper.

b. Dip each ladyfinger quickly into a mixture of strawberry jam and water. Arrange them around the sides of the pan, pressing them against the parchment paper.

c. Place a layer of ladyfingers on the bottom of the pan.

5. Assemble the Charlotte:

a. Pour half of the strawberry mousse over the ladyfinger base.

b. Add another layer of ladyfingers on top of the mousse.

c. Pour the remaining strawberry mousse over the second layer of ladyfingers.

d. Smooth the top with a spatula.

6. Chill:

a. Refrigerate the Strawberry Charlotte for at least 4 hours or until set.

7. Garnish and Serve:

a. Once set, remove the springform pan and parchment paper from the sides.

b. Garnish the top with fresh strawberries, mint leaves, and a dusting of powdered sugar if desired.

c. Slice and serve chilled.

A Strawberry Charlotte is a refreshing and elegant dessert, perfect for special occasions or a delightful summer treat. Enjoy the combination of light strawberry mousse and the delicate texture of ladyfingers!

Profiteroles with Salted Caramel Sauce

Ingredients:

For the Choux Pastry:

- 1 cup water
- 1/2 cup unsalted butter
- 1/4 teaspoon salt
- 1 cup all-purpose flour
- 4 large eggs

For the Filling:

- Vanilla ice cream or sweetened whipped cream

For the Salted Caramel Sauce:

- 1 cup granulated sugar
- 6 tablespoons unsalted butter, cut into pieces
- 1/2 cup heavy cream
- 1 teaspoon sea salt (adjust to taste)

Instructions:

1. Preheat the Oven:

a. Preheat your oven to 425°F (220°C). Line a baking sheet with parchment paper.

2. Make the Choux Pastry:

a. In a medium saucepan, combine water, butter, and salt. Bring to a boil over medium heat.

b. Reduce heat to low and add the flour all at once. Stir vigorously with a wooden spoon until the mixture forms a ball and pulls away from the sides of the pan.

c. Remove from heat and let it cool for a few minutes.

d. Add the eggs one at a time, beating well after each addition. Make sure each egg is fully incorporated before adding the next. The dough should become smooth and glossy.

e. Transfer the choux pastry dough to a piping bag fitted with a large round tip.

3. Pipe and Bake:

a. Pipe small mounds of the choux pastry onto the prepared baking sheet, leaving space between each.

b. Bake in the preheated oven for 15 minutes, then reduce the temperature to 375°F (190°C) and continue baking for an additional 15-20 minutes or until the profiteroles are golden brown and puffed.

c. Remove from the oven and let them cool completely.

4. Prepare the Filling:

a. Once the profiteroles are cool, cut them in half horizontally.

b. Fill each profiterole with a scoop of vanilla ice cream or sweetened whipped cream.

5. Make the Salted Caramel Sauce:

a. In a heavy-bottomed saucepan, heat the granulated sugar over medium heat. Stir continuously until the sugar melts and turns into a golden caramel.

b. Add the butter, stirring continuously until it's fully melted into the caramel.

c. Slowly pour in the heavy cream while stirring. Be careful, as the mixture may bubble.

d. Continue to stir until the sauce is smooth and well combined.

e. Remove from heat and stir in the sea salt. Adjust the salt to taste.

6. Drizzle with Salted Caramel Sauce:

a. Drizzle the salted caramel sauce over the filled profiteroles.

7. Serve:

a. Serve the Profiteroles with Salted Caramel Sauce immediately while the caramel is still warm.

Enjoy these delightful profiteroles with a perfect combination of crisp choux pastry, creamy filling, and rich salted caramel sauce!

Crème Brûlée

Ingredients:

- 2 cups heavy cream
- 1 vanilla bean, split lengthwise (or 1 tablespoon pure vanilla extract)
- 5 large egg yolks
- 1/2 cup granulated sugar, plus extra for caramelizing the top

Instructions:

1. Preheat the Oven:

a. Preheat your oven to 325°F (160°C). Place ramekins in a deep baking dish.

2. Infuse the Cream:

a. In a saucepan, heat the heavy cream and vanilla bean (or vanilla extract) over medium heat until it just starts to simmer. Do not let it boil.

b. Remove from heat and let it sit for a few minutes to allow the vanilla to infuse into the cream.

3. Prepare the Egg Mixture:

a. In a mixing bowl, whisk together the egg yolks and sugar until well combined.

b. Gradually pour the warm cream into the egg mixture while whisking continuously to avoid curdling.

4. Strain the Mixture:

a. Strain the custard mixture through a fine-mesh sieve into a clean bowl to remove the vanilla bean and any potential bits of cooked egg.

5. Fill the Ramekins:

a. Divide the custard mixture evenly among the ramekins.

6. Bake in a Water Bath:

a. Place the baking dish with the filled ramekins in the preheated oven.

b. Pour hot water into the baking dish to create a water bath, surrounding the ramekins. Be careful not to get water into the custard.

7. Bake the Custard:

a. Bake for approximately 35-40 minutes or until the custard is set but still slightly jiggly in the center.

8. Chill:

a. Remove the ramekins from the water bath and let them cool to room temperature.

b. Once cooled, refrigerate the custard for at least 4 hours, or overnight, to allow it to firm up.

9. Caramelize the Sugar:

a. Just before serving, sprinkle a thin, even layer of granulated sugar on top of each custard.

b. Use a kitchen torch to caramelize the sugar until it forms a golden-brown crust. If you don't have a kitchen torch, you can use the broiler setting in your oven, but be sure to watch closely to avoid burning.

10. Serve:

a. Allow the sugar to cool and harden for a minute or two before serving.

b. Serve the Crème Brûlée with the crunchy caramelized top.

Enjoy the creamy, decadent delight of homemade Crème Brûlée with its contrasting textures of smooth custard and crisp caramelized sugar.

Kouign-Amann

Ingredients:

For the Dough:

- 2 1/4 teaspoons (1 packet) active dry yeast
- 1 1/4 cups warm milk
- 3 1/2 cups all-purpose flour, plus extra for dusting
- 1 teaspoon salt
- 1 cup (2 sticks) unsalted butter, cold, cut into small pieces

For the Filling:

- 1 cup granulated sugar, plus extra for rolling
- Additional cold unsalted butter for folding

Instructions:

1. Activate the Yeast:

a. In a bowl, combine the warm milk and yeast. Let it sit for about 5 minutes until it becomes frothy.

2. Make the Dough:

a. In a large mixing bowl, combine the flour and salt.

b. Add the yeast mixture to the flour and mix until a dough forms.

c. Knead the dough on a floured surface for about 5 minutes until smooth.

d. Roll the dough into a rectangle, then cover it with plastic wrap and refrigerate for 30 minutes.

3. Incorporate the Butter:

a. Roll out the chilled dough into a rectangle.

b. Dot the surface of the dough with cold butter pieces and fold it in thirds, like a letter.

c. Roll out the folded dough into a rectangle again, then fold it in thirds once more.

d. Wrap the dough in plastic wrap and refrigerate for another 30 minutes.

4. Layer with Sugar:

a. Roll out the chilled dough into a rectangle again.

b. Sprinkle the entire surface with granulated sugar and fold it in thirds.

c. Wrap the dough and refrigerate for an additional 30 minutes.

5. Shape the Kouign-Amann:

a. Preheat your oven to 375°F (190°C).

b. Roll out the dough into a large rectangle.

c. Sprinkle the surface with more granulated sugar.

d. Cut the dough into squares or rectangles.

e. Place each square or rectangle into a well-buttered muffin tin or on a baking sheet.

6. Bake:

a. Bake in the preheated oven for about 25-30 minutes or until the Kouign-Amann is golden brown and caramelized.

7. Cool and Enjoy:

a. Allow the Kouign-Amann to cool slightly before removing them from the muffin tin or baking sheet.

b. Enjoy these delightful pastries warm or at room temperature.

Kouign-Amann is a delightful treat that combines the richness of butter with layers of caramelized sugar, resulting in a flaky and sweet pastry. It's perfect for breakfast, brunch, or as a special treat with your favorite hot beverage.

Cherry Pistachio Galette

Ingredients:

For the Dough:

- 1 1/4 cups all-purpose flour
- 1 tablespoon granulated sugar
- 1/2 cup unsalted butter, cold and cut into small pieces
- 1/4 cup ice water
- A pinch of salt

For the Filling:

- 2 cups fresh cherries, pitted and halved
- 1/4 cup granulated sugar (adjust based on the sweetness of cherries)
- 1 tablespoon cornstarch
- 1/4 cup chopped pistachios
- 1 tablespoon honey or maple syrup (for brushing)

For Assembly:

- 1 egg (for egg wash)
- Powdered sugar (for dusting, optional)
- Extra chopped pistachios (for garnish, optional)
- Vanilla ice cream (optional, for serving)

Instructions:

1. Make the Dough:

a. In a food processor, combine the flour, sugar, and salt.

b. Add the cold butter pieces and pulse until the mixture resembles coarse crumbs.

c. Gradually add the ice water and pulse just until the dough comes together.

d. Turn the dough out onto a floured surface, shape it into a disk, wrap in plastic wrap, and refrigerate for at least 30 minutes.

2. Preheat the Oven:

a. Preheat your oven to 375°F (190°C). Line a baking sheet with parchment paper.

3. Prepare the Filling:

a. In a bowl, toss the halved cherries with sugar and cornstarch until well coated. Let it sit for a few minutes.

4. Roll Out the Dough:

a. On a floured surface, roll out the chilled dough into a rough circle, about 12 inches in diameter.

5. Assemble the Galette:

a. Transfer the rolled-out dough onto the prepared baking sheet.

b. Arrange the sugared cherries in the center of the dough, leaving a border around the edges.

c. Sprinkle chopped pistachios over the cherries.

d. Gently fold the edges of the dough over the filling, creating pleats and leaving the center exposed.

6. Egg Wash:

a. Beat the egg and brush it over the edges of the galette for a golden finish.

7. Bake:

a. Bake in the preheated oven for about 35-40 minutes or until the crust is golden brown and the cherries are bubbling.

8. Glaze and Garnish:

a. While the galette is still warm, brush the exposed cherries with honey or maple syrup for a shiny glaze.

b. Optionally, dust the galette with powdered sugar and sprinkle extra chopped pistachios on top.

9. Serve:

a. Allow the Cherry Pistachio Galette to cool slightly before slicing.

b. Serve slices with a scoop of vanilla ice cream if desired.

This Cherry Pistachio Galette is a delightful combination of sweet cherries, crunchy pistachios, and buttery, flaky crust. It's a versatile and easy-to-make dessert that captures the essence of summer. Enjoy it on its own or with a dollop of whipped cream or ice cream.

Brioche aux Pralines

Ingredients:

For the Brioche:

- 3 1/4 cups all-purpose flour
- 1/4 cup granulated sugar
- 1 teaspoon salt
- 1 packet (2 1/4 teaspoons) active dry yeast
- 1/2 cup warm milk
- 4 large eggs
- 1 cup unsalted butter, softened

For the Pralines:

- 1 cup whole almonds or hazelnuts
- 1 cup granulated sugar

Instructions:

Prepare the Brioche Dough:

a. In a bowl, combine the warm milk and active dry yeast. Let it sit for about 5 minutes until it becomes frothy.

b. In a large mixing bowl, combine the flour, sugar, and salt.

c. Make a well in the center of the dry ingredients and add the frothy yeast mixture.

d. Add the eggs one at a time, mixing well after each addition.

e. Gradually incorporate the softened butter and knead the dough until it becomes smooth and elastic.

> f. Cover the bowl with a clean kitchen towel and let the dough rise in a warm place for about 1-2 hours, or until it has doubled in size.

Prepare the Pralines:

a. In a dry skillet over medium heat, toast the almonds or hazelnuts until lightly browned and fragrant. Remove from heat and let them cool.

b. In a saucepan, melt the sugar over medium heat until it becomes a golden caramel. Be careful not to burn it.

c. Add the toasted nuts to the caramel, stirring quickly to coat them evenly.

    d. Transfer the praline mixture to a parchment-lined baking sheet and let it cool completely. Once cooled, break it into small pieces.

Assemble the Brioche aux Pralines:

a. Preheat your oven to 350°F (175°C).

b. Punch down the risen brioche dough and divide it in half.

c. Roll out one portion of the dough into a rectangle and sprinkle half of the praline pieces over it.

d. Roll the dough into a log, sealing the edges.

e. Repeat the process with the remaining dough and pralines.

f. Place the rolled brioche logs in greased loaf pans and let them rise for an additional 30 minutes.

    g. Bake in the preheated oven for about 25-30 minutes or until the brioche is golden brown and sounds hollow when tapped on the bottom.

Serve:

    a. Allow the Brioche aux Pralines to cool slightly before slicing and serving.

Enjoy your delicious Brioche aux Pralines!

Pain d'Épices (Spice Bread)

Ingredients:

- 2 cups all-purpose flour
- 1/2 cup rye flour
- 1 teaspoon baking powder
- 1/2 teaspoon baking soda
- 1/2 teaspoon salt
- 1 teaspoon ground cinnamon
- 1/2 teaspoon ground ginger
- 1/4 teaspoon ground cloves
- 1/4 teaspoon ground nutmeg
- 1/2 cup unsalted butter, softened
- 1/2 cup honey
- 1/2 cup molasses
- 1 cup buttermilk
- 1/4 cup orange zest (optional)

Instructions:

Preheat the Oven:

Preheat your oven to 350°F (175°C). Grease and flour a loaf pan.

Combine Dry Ingredients:

In a large bowl, whisk together the all-purpose flour, rye flour, baking powder, baking soda, salt, and the ground spices (cinnamon, ginger, cloves, nutmeg).

Prepare Wet Ingredients:

In another bowl, cream together the softened butter, honey, and molasses until well combined.

Combine Wet and Dry Ingredients:

Add the wet ingredients to the dry ingredients and mix until just combined. Gradually add the buttermilk and continue to mix until a smooth batter forms. If desired, fold in the orange zest for extra flavor.

Bake the Spice Bread:

Pour the batter into the prepared loaf pan. Smooth the top with a spatula. Bake in the preheated oven for approximately 45-55 minutes, or until a toothpick inserted into the center comes out clean.

Cool and Serve:

Allow the Pain d'Épices to cool in the pan for about 10 minutes before transferring it to a wire rack to cool completely. Once cooled, slice and serve.

Optional Glaze:

You can optionally drizzle the cooled spice bread with a simple glaze made with powdered sugar and a small amount of milk for added sweetness.

Enjoy your homemade Pain d'Épices with a cup of tea or coffee!

Macarons

Ingredients:

For the Macaron Shells:

- 1 cup (100g) almond flour
- 1 3/4 cups (200g) confectioners' sugar
- 3 large egg whites, at room temperature
- 1/4 cup (50g) granulated sugar
- Gel food coloring (optional)

For the Filling:

- 1/2 cup (113g) unsalted butter, softened
- 1 cup (120g) confectioners' sugar
- Flavoring of your choice (vanilla extract, fruit extracts, etc.)

Instructions:

Prepare Baking Sheets:

Line two baking sheets with parchment paper or silicone mats.

Make Almond Flour Mixture:

In a food processor, combine almond flour and confectioners' sugar. Pulse until well combined and fine in texture. Sift the mixture into a large bowl to remove any lumps.

Whip Egg Whites:

In a clean, dry bowl, whip the egg whites using an electric mixer until they become foamy. Gradually add granulated sugar while continuing to whip. Whip until stiff peaks form. If using food coloring, add it at this point and gently fold it into the meringue.

Macaronage:

Carefully fold the almond flour mixture into the whipped egg whites using a spatula. This step is crucial - you want to achieve a smooth, shiny batter with a lava-like consistency. Be gentle to preserve the airiness of the meringue.

Pipe Macarons:

Transfer the batter into a piping bag fitted with a round tip. Pipe small, uniform circles onto the prepared baking sheets, leaving space between each macaron shell.

Resting Time:

Let the piped macarons sit at room temperature for about 20-30 minutes. This helps them develop a skin, which is essential for the characteristic "feet" to form during baking.

Preheat Oven:

Preheat your oven to 300°F (150°C).

Bake:

Bake the macarons for 15-18 minutes, or until they have developed a crisp shell and the characteristic "feet." The exact time may vary, so keep a close eye on them.

Make the Filling:

While the macarons are baking, prepare the filling. Cream together softened butter, confectioners' sugar, and your chosen flavoring until smooth.

Assemble:

Once the macarons have cooled, match up similar-sized shells and pipe or spoon a small amount of filling onto one shell. Gently press another shell on top to create a sandwich.

Mature:

Place the assembled macarons in an airtight container and refrigerate for 24-48 hours. This allows the flavors to meld and the texture to improve.

Serve:

Bring the macarons to room temperature before serving for the best taste and texture.

Enjoy your homemade macarons! They make a perfect indulgence for special occasions or as a delightful treat any time.

Pissaladière

Ingredients:

For the Dough:

- 2 1/2 cups (320g) all-purpose flour
- 1 teaspoon salt
- 1 teaspoon sugar
- 1 cup (240ml) warm water
- 1 packet (2 1/4 teaspoons) active dry yeast
- 2 tablespoons olive oil

For the Topping:

- 3 tablespoons olive oil
- 4 large onions, thinly sliced
- 2 cloves garlic, minced
- 1 teaspoon dried thyme
- Salt and black pepper to taste
- 1 can (2 ounces) anchovy fillets, drained
- 1/2 cup black olives, such as Niçoise olives or Kalamata olives, pitted and halved

Instructions:

For the Dough:

Activate the Yeast:

In a small bowl, combine warm water, sugar, and yeast. Let it sit for about 5-10 minutes until it becomes frothy.

Mix the Dough:

In a large bowl, combine the flour and salt. Make a well in the center and add the activated yeast mixture and olive oil. Mix until a dough forms.

Knead and Rise:

Turn the dough out onto a floured surface and knead for about 5-7 minutes, or until the dough is smooth and elastic. Place it in a lightly oiled bowl, cover with a clean kitchen towel, and let it rise in a warm place for 1-2 hours or until doubled in size.

For the Topping:

Caramelize the Onions:

In a large skillet, heat olive oil over medium heat. Add the sliced onions, minced garlic, thyme, salt, and black pepper. Cook, stirring occasionally, until the onions are soft and caramelized, about 20-25 minutes.

Preheat Oven:

Preheat your oven to 400°F (200°C).

Roll Out the Dough:

Punch down the risen dough and roll it out on a floured surface to fit a baking sheet. Transfer the rolled-out dough to a parchment-lined or greased baking sheet.

Assemble:

Spread the caramelized onions evenly over the rolled-out dough. Arrange the anchovy fillets in a crisscross pattern on top of the onions. Place the olive halves between the anchovies.

Bake:

Bake in the preheated oven for 20-25 minutes or until the edges of the dough are golden brown.

Serve:

Allow the Pissaladière to cool for a few minutes before slicing and serving. It can be served warm or at room temperature.

Pissaladière is a great appetizer or light meal, and it's perfect for gatherings or picnics. Enjoy the rich flavors of caramelized onions, briny anchovies, and olives in this classic Provençal dish!

Flan Parisien

Ingredients:

For the Pastry:

- 2 cups (250g) all-purpose flour
- 1 cup (225g) unsalted butter, cold and cut into small cubes
- 1/4 cup (50g) granulated sugar
- 1/4 teaspoon salt
- 1 large egg
- 2 tablespoons ice water

For the Custard Filling:

- 2 cups (480ml) whole milk
- 1 vanilla bean or 1 teaspoon vanilla extract
- 1 cup (200g) granulated sugar
- 1/2 cup (60g) cornstarch
- 4 large egg yolks
- 2 tablespoons unsalted butter

Instructions:

For the Pastry:

Prepare the Dough:

In a food processor, combine the flour, sugar, and salt. Add the cold, cubed butter and pulse until the mixture resembles coarse crumbs.

Add Egg and Water:

Add the egg to the mixture and pulse again. Gradually add ice water, one tablespoon at a time, until the dough just comes together. Be careful not to overmix.

Chill the Dough:

Turn the dough out onto a floured surface, shape it into a disk, wrap it in plastic wrap, and refrigerate for at least 1 hour.

Roll Out the Dough:

Preheat your oven to 375°F (190°C). Roll out the chilled dough on a floured surface to fit a tart pan. Press the dough into the pan, trim the edges, and prick the bottom with a fork. Line the pastry with parchment paper and fill it with pie weights or dried beans.

Blind Bake:

Blind bake the crust in the preheated oven for about 15 minutes. Remove the parchment paper and weights, and bake for an additional 5-10 minutes or until the crust is golden brown. Allow it to cool while preparing the custard filling.

For the Custard Filling:

Prepare Vanilla Infusion:

In a saucepan, heat the milk over medium heat until it is warm. If using a vanilla bean, split it open, scrape the seeds into the milk, and add the pod. If using vanilla extract, add it directly to the milk. Heat until almost boiling, then remove from heat and let it steep for about 10-15 minutes.

Mix Sugar and Cornstarch:

In a separate bowl, whisk together sugar and cornstarch.

Whisk in Egg Yolks:

Whisk the egg yolks into the sugar and cornstarch mixture until well combined.

Combine:

Gradually pour the warm milk into the egg mixture, whisking constantly. Remove the vanilla bean pod if used.

Cook the Custard:

Transfer the mixture back to the saucepan and cook over medium heat, whisking continuously, until the custard thickens. This may take around 5-7 minutes.

Add Butter:

> Remove the custard from heat, add the butter, and stir until it is fully incorporated.

Fill the Pastry:

> Pour the custard into the pre-baked pastry crust and smooth the top.

Chill:

> Allow the Flan Parisien to cool to room temperature, then refrigerate for at least 2-3 hours or until fully chilled and set.

Serve:

> Once chilled, slice the Flan Parisien and serve. Optionally, you can dust the top with powdered sugar or add a light caramelized sugar crust using a kitchen torch.

Enjoy the creamy, vanilla-infused goodness of this classic French custard tart!

Almond Croissants

Ingredients:

For the Croissants:

- 1 sheet of puff pastry (store-bought or homemade)
- 1/2 cup (1 stick or 113g) unsalted butter, chilled but pliable
- 1 egg (for egg wash)
- Powdered sugar (for dusting, optional)

For the Almond Filling:

- 1 cup (100g) almond flour
- 1/2 cup (100g) granulated sugar
- 1/4 cup (60g) unsalted butter, softened
- 1 large egg
- 1 teaspoon almond extract
- Sliced almonds for topping

For Simple Syrup (optional):

- 1/4 cup (60ml) water
- 1/4 cup (50g) granulated sugar

Instructions:

For the Almond Filling:

Make Almond Filling:

In a bowl, mix together almond flour, granulated sugar, softened butter, egg, and almond extract until well combined. Set aside.

For the Croissants:

Preheat Oven:

Preheat your oven to 375°F (190°C).

Roll Out the Puff Pastry:

Roll out the puff pastry sheet on a lightly floured surface. If it's not pre-rolled, aim for a rectangle about 1/8 inch thick.

Spread Butter:

Spread the chilled but pliable butter over two-thirds of the pastry, leaving one-third without butter.

Fold the Pastry:

Fold the unbuttered third over the middle third, then fold the other third over the first, creating three layers. This process is known as a "letter fold."

Roll and Chill:

Roll out the folded pastry to the original size and thickness, then fold it again. Wrap it in plastic wrap and chill it in the refrigerator for about 30 minutes.

Repeat:

Repeat the rolling and folding process two more times, chilling the dough between each turn. This creates layers and helps achieve a flaky texture.

Prepare Almond Croissants:

After the final chilling, roll out the dough one more time. Cut the dough into triangles.

Add Almond Filling:

Place a spoonful of almond filling at the base of each triangle and roll them up, starting from the base and tucking the edges underneath.

Egg Wash:

Beat the egg and brush it over the tops of the croissants for a golden finish.

Bake:

Place the almond croissants on a baking sheet lined with parchment paper and bake for about 15-20 minutes or until golden brown and puffed.

Optional Simple Syrup:

Make Simple Syrup (Optional):

In a saucepan, heat water and sugar until the sugar dissolves. Brush the warm syrup over the baked almond croissants for a shiny finish.

Serve:

Allow the almond croissants to cool slightly before serving. Optionally, dust with powdered sugar before serving.

Enjoy your homemade Almond Croissants with their flaky layers and delicious almond filling!

Tarte au Citron (Lemon Tart)

Ingredients:

For the Tart Crust:

- 1 1/4 cups (160g) all-purpose flour
- 1/2 cup (60g) powdered sugar
- 1/2 cup (1 stick or 113g) unsalted butter, chilled and cut into small cubes
- 1 large egg yolk
- 1-2 tablespoons ice water

For the Lemon Filling:

- 4-5 large lemons (for zest and juice)
- 1 cup (200g) granulated sugar
- 1/2 cup (1 stick or 113g) unsalted butter, melted
- 4 large eggs
- 1 teaspoon vanilla extract
- Pinch of salt

For Garnish (Optional):

- Powdered sugar
- Lemon zest
- Fresh berries or mint leaves

Instructions:

For the Tart Crust:

Prepare the Crust:

> In a food processor, combine the flour and powdered sugar. Add the chilled butter cubes and pulse until the mixture resembles coarse crumbs.

Add Egg Yolk and Water:

> Add the egg yolk and 1-2 tablespoons of ice water. Pulse until the dough comes together. If needed, add more water, one tablespoon at a time.

Form a Disk:

Turn the dough out onto a floured surface and gently knead it to form a smooth disk. Wrap it in plastic wrap and refrigerate for at least 30 minutes.

Preheat Oven:

Preheat your oven to 375°F (190°C).

Roll Out the Dough:

Roll out the chilled dough on a floured surface to fit your tart pan. Press the dough into the pan, ensuring it covers the bottom and sides evenly. Trim any excess dough.

Blind Bake:

Line the tart crust with parchment paper and fill it with pie weights or dried beans. Blind bake for 15 minutes. Remove the weights and parchment, then bake for an additional 5-7 minutes, or until the crust is golden. Allow it to cool while you prepare the filling.

For the Lemon Filling:

Prepare Lemon Zest and Juice:

Zest the lemons and squeeze enough juice to yield 1 cup.

Make Lemon Filling:

In a bowl, whisk together the granulated sugar, melted butter, eggs, lemon zest, lemon juice, vanilla extract, and a pinch of salt until well combined.

Pour Filling into Crust:

Pour the lemon filling into the pre-baked tart crust.

Bake:

Bake the tart in the preheated oven for 20-25 minutes or until the filling is set and has a slight jiggle in the center.

Cool:

Allow the lemon tart to cool completely on a wire rack.

Garnish and Serve:

Optionally, garnish the tart with powdered sugar, additional lemon zest, and fresh berries or mint leaves. Slice and serve.

Enjoy your delicious homemade Tarte au Citron! Its bright and zesty flavor makes it a perfect dessert for any occasion.

Pâte Sablée Tart Shells

Ingredients:

- 1 1/4 cups (160g) all-purpose flour
- 1/3 cup (40g) powdered sugar
- 1/2 cup (1 stick or 113g) unsalted butter, chilled and cut into small cubes
- 1 large egg yolk
- 1 teaspoon vanilla extract
- Pinch of salt

Instructions:

Prepare Ingredients:

    Ensure all ingredients are cold, and the butter is cut into small cubes.

Combine Flour and Sugar:

    In a food processor, combine the all-purpose flour and powdered sugar. Pulse a few times to mix.

Add Butter:

    Add the chilled, cubed butter to the flour mixture. Pulse until the mixture resembles coarse crumbs and the butter is distributed evenly.

Add Egg Yolk and Vanilla:

    Add the egg yolk and vanilla extract to the mixture. Pulse until the dough starts to come together. Be careful not to over-process.

Form the Dough:

    Turn the mixture out onto a lightly floured surface. Gently knead the dough until it forms a cohesive ball. Flatten the ball into a disk.

Chill the Dough:

Wrap the dough in plastic wrap and refrigerate for at least 30 minutes to 1 hour. This chilling process allows the butter to firm up and makes the dough easier to handle.

Preheat Oven:

Preheat your oven to 375°F (190°C).

Roll Out the Dough:

On a floured surface, roll out the chilled dough to your desired thickness, usually around 1/8 to 1/4 inch.

Cut and Shape Tart Shells:

Cut out circles of dough using a round cookie cutter or a glass that is slightly larger than your tart molds. Gently press the dough circles into the tart molds, ensuring an even layer on the bottom and up the sides.

Prick the Bottoms:

Prick the bottoms of the tart shells with a fork. This prevents the dough from puffing up too much during baking.

Chill Again:

Place the filled tart molds in the refrigerator for another 15-20 minutes to firm up the dough.

Bake:

Bake the tart shells in the preheated oven for about 12-15 minutes or until they are golden brown.

Cool:

Allow the tart shells to cool completely in the molds before removing them.

Now, your Pâte Sablée Tart Shells are ready to be filled with your favorite pastry cream, fruit compote, or any other delicious filling of your choice. Enjoy creating delightful tarts with this sweet and crumbly pastry!

Chausson aux Pommes (Apple Turnovers)

Ingredients:

For the Apple Filling:

- 2 medium-sized apples, peeled, cored, and diced
- 2 tablespoons unsalted butter
- 1/4 cup (50g) granulated sugar
- 1/2 teaspoon ground cinnamon
- 1/4 teaspoon ground nutmeg
- 1 tablespoon all-purpose flour
- 1 teaspoon lemon juice

For the Pastry:

- 1 package (about 17.3 ounces or 490g) puff pastry sheets, thawed if frozen
- Flour for dusting
- 1 egg, beaten (for egg wash)
- Powdered sugar for dusting (optional)

Instructions:

Preheat Oven:

Preheat your oven to 400°F (200°C).

Prepare Apple Filling:

In a saucepan over medium heat, melt the butter. Add the diced apples and cook for about 2-3 minutes until they begin to soften.

Add Sugar and Spices:

Stir in the granulated sugar, ground cinnamon, ground nutmeg, and all-purpose flour. Cook for an additional 3-4 minutes until the apples are tender and coated in the spiced sugar mixture.

Add Lemon Juice:

Remove the saucepan from heat and stir in the lemon juice. Allow the apple filling to cool while you prepare the pastry.

Roll Out the Pastry:

On a floured surface, roll out the puff pastry sheets to about 1/8-inch thickness. If using pre-rolled sheets, ensure they are evenly rolled.

Cut into Squares:

Cut the rolled-out pastry into squares of your desired size. A common size is around 4 to 6 inches.

Add Apple Filling:

Place a spoonful of the cooled apple filling in the center of each pastry square.

Fold and Seal:

Fold the pastry over the filling to create a triangle or rectangle shape, then press the edges to seal. You can use a fork to crimp the edges for a decorative touch.

Brush with Egg Wash:

Brush the tops of the turnovers with beaten egg. This gives them a golden and shiny finish when baked.

Bake:

Place the filled turnovers on a parchment-lined baking sheet and bake in the preheated oven for 15-20 minutes or until they are puffed and golden brown.

Cool and Dust with Powdered Sugar:

Allow the Chausson aux Pommes to cool slightly before serving. Optionally, dust with powdered sugar for an extra touch of sweetness.

Serve:

Serve the apple turnovers warm and enjoy!

Chausson aux Pommes are perfect for breakfast, brunch, or as a delicious dessert. The combination of flaky pastry and spiced apple filling is sure to delight your taste buds.

Dark Chocolate Tarte Tatin

Ingredients:

For the Dark Chocolate Layer:

- 4 ounces (about 115g) dark chocolate, chopped
- 2 tablespoons unsalted butter

For the Caramelized Apples:

- 4-5 medium-sized apples (such as Granny Smith), peeled, cored, and sliced
- 1/2 cup (1 stick or 113g) unsalted butter
- 1 cup (200g) granulated sugar
- 1 teaspoon vanilla extract

For the Pastry:

- 1 sheet puff pastry, thawed if frozen

Instructions:

Preheat Oven:

Preheat your oven to 375°F (190°C).

Prepare the Dark Chocolate Layer:

In a small saucepan over low heat, melt the dark chocolate and 2 tablespoons of butter. Stir until smooth and well combined. Remove from heat and set aside.

Caramelize the Apples:

In an oven-safe skillet (preferably cast iron), melt 1/2 cup of butter over medium heat. Add the granulated sugar and vanilla extract. Stir until the sugar dissolves and the mixture begins to caramelize, turning a golden brown color.

Add Apple Slices:

Add the sliced apples to the caramel, ensuring they are evenly coated. Cook for about 5-7 minutes, stirring occasionally, until the apples are slightly softened and caramelized. Remove from heat.

Add Dark Chocolate Layer:

Spoon the melted dark chocolate over the caramelized apples, spreading it evenly.

Roll Out Puff Pastry:

Roll out the puff pastry on a floured surface to fit the size of your skillet.

Cover Apples with Pastry:

Place the puff pastry over the apples and tuck in the edges around the apples to encase them.

Bake:

Transfer the skillet to the preheated oven and bake for 20-25 minutes or until the puff pastry is golden brown and cooked through.

Invert the Tarte Tatin:

Remove the skillet from the oven and let it cool for a couple of minutes. Carefully invert the Dark Chocolate Tarte Tatin onto a serving plate.

Serve:

Serve the Dark Chocolate Tarte Tatin warm, either on its own or with a scoop of vanilla ice cream for an extra indulgence.

Enjoy the rich combination of dark chocolate, caramelized apples, and buttery puff pastry in this delightful dessert!

Raspberry Rose Choux au Craquelin

Ingredients:

For the Choux Pastry:

- 1/2 cup (120ml) water
- 1/2 cup (120ml) whole milk
- 1/2 cup (1 stick or 113g) unsalted butter, cut into small pieces
- 1 tablespoon granulated sugar
- 1/4 teaspoon salt
- 1 cup (125g) all-purpose flour
- 4 large eggs, at room temperature

For the Craquelin:

- 1/2 cup (65g) all-purpose flour
- 1/4 cup (50g) granulated sugar
- 3 tablespoons unsalted butter, softened
- 1-2 drops pink food coloring (optional)

For the Raspberry Rose Filling:

- 1 cup fresh raspberries
- 1/4 cup granulated sugar
- 1 teaspoon rose water
- 1 cup heavy cream, chilled
- Powdered sugar for dusting (optional)

Instructions:

For the Choux Pastry:

Preheat Oven:

Preheat your oven to 400°F (200°C). Line a baking sheet with parchment paper.

Make Choux Dough:

In a saucepan, combine water, milk, butter, sugar, and salt. Bring to a boil over medium heat. Remove from heat and add the flour all at once. Stir vigorously until the mixture comes together.

Cook the Dough:

Return the saucepan to low heat and continue stirring for about 2-3 minutes to cook the dough slightly. Transfer the dough to a mixing bowl and let it cool for a few minutes.

Add Eggs:

Add the eggs one at a time, beating well after each addition. The dough should be smooth, shiny, and hold its shape.

Pipe Choux:

Transfer the choux pastry to a piping bag fitted with a large round tip. Pipe small mounds onto the prepared baking sheet, leaving space between each.

For the Craquelin:

Make Craquelin Dough:

In a bowl, combine flour, sugar, softened butter, and food coloring (if using). Mix until you get a smooth, homogeneous dough.

Roll Out Craquelin:

Roll out the craquelin dough between two sheets of parchment paper to about 1/8-inch thickness. Use a round cookie cutter to cut circles slightly smaller than the choux mounds.

Top Choux with Craquelin:

Place a craquelin disc on top of each choux mound.

Bake:

Bake in the preheated oven for 15-20 minutes or until the choux are puffed and golden brown. Reduce the heat to 350°F (180°C) and bake for an additional 10 minutes to ensure they are cooked through.

Cool:

Allow the choux to cool completely on a wire rack.

For the Raspberry Rose Filling:

Prepare Raspberry Puree:

In a blender or food processor, blend fresh raspberries until smooth. Strain the puree to remove seeds.

Make Raspberry Rose Filling:

In a bowl, combine raspberry puree, granulated sugar, and rose water. In a separate bowl, whip the chilled heavy cream until stiff peaks form. Gently fold the raspberry mixture into the whipped cream.

Fill the Choux:

Slice the choux in half horizontally. Fill each bottom half with the raspberry rose cream. Place the other half on top.

Dust with Powdered Sugar:

Dust the Raspberry Rose Choux au Craquelin with powdered sugar before serving.

Enjoy these elegant and delicious Raspberry Rose Choux au Craquelin as a delightful treat for special occasions or celebrations!

Pineapple Coconut Opera Cake

Ingredients:

For the Almond Sponge Cake:

- 1 cup (100g) almond flour
- 1 cup (125g) powdered sugar
- 3 large eggs, room temperature
- 2 large egg yolks, room temperature
- 1/4 cup (30g) all-purpose flour
- 2 tablespoons unsalted butter, melted

For the Coffee Syrup:

- 1/2 cup strong coffee, cooled
- 1/4 cup sugar

For the Pineapple Coconut Ganache:

- 8 ounces (225g) white chocolate, finely chopped
- 1/3 cup coconut cream
- 1/4 cup pineapple puree

For the Pineapple Coconut Buttercream:

- 1 cup (225g) unsalted butter, softened
- 2 cups (250g) powdered sugar
- 1/4 cup coconut cream
- 1/4 cup pineapple puree

For Assembly:

- Toasted coconut flakes (for decoration)
- Pineapple chunks (for decoration)

Instructions:

For the Almond Sponge Cake:

Preheat Oven:

Preheat your oven to 350°F (180°C). Grease and line a baking sheet with parchment paper.

Prepare Almond Sponge Batter:

In a bowl, whisk together almond flour and powdered sugar. In another bowl, whisk together eggs, egg yolks, and all-purpose flour until well combined. Gently fold in the almond flour mixture. Add melted butter and fold until smooth.

Bake:

Spread the batter evenly onto the prepared baking sheet. Bake for 10-12 minutes or until the sponge is set and lightly browned. Let it cool.

For the Coffee Syrup:

Make Coffee Syrup:

In a small saucepan, combine strong coffee and sugar. Bring to a simmer, stirring until the sugar dissolves. Remove from heat and let it cool.

For the Pineapple Coconut Ganache:

Prepare Pineapple Coconut Ganache:

Place finely chopped white chocolate in a heatproof bowl. In a saucepan, heat coconut cream and pineapple puree until hot but not boiling. Pour over the white chocolate and let it sit for a minute. Stir until smooth. Let it cool.

For the Pineapple Coconut Buttercream:

Make Pineapple Coconut Buttercream:

In a bowl, beat softened butter until creamy. Add powdered sugar, coconut cream, and pineapple puree. Beat until smooth and fluffy.

For Assembly:

Cut Almond Sponge:

Cut the cooled almond sponge into three equal-sized rectangles.

Assemble Layers:

Place one layer of almond sponge in the bottom of a lined cake pan. Brush with coffee syrup. Spread a layer of pineapple-coconut ganache, followed by a layer of pineapple coconut buttercream. Repeat with the remaining layers.

Chill:

Chill the assembled cake in the refrigerator for at least 4 hours or overnight.

Decorate:

Before serving, decorate the Pineapple Coconut Opera Cake with toasted coconut flakes and pineapple chunks.

Slice and Serve:

Slice and serve the Pineapple Coconut Opera Cake. Enjoy the tropical flavors!

This Pineapple Coconut Opera Cake combines the richness of almond sponge, the sweetness of pineapple and coconut, and the coffee undertones for a delightful dessert experience.

Lemon Verbena Madeleines

Ingredients:

- 2 tablespoons fresh lemon verbena leaves, finely chopped
- 3 large eggs, at room temperature
- 2/3 cup (130g) granulated sugar
- 1 cup (125g) all-purpose flour
- 1 teaspoon baking powder
- 1/2 cup (1 stick or 113g) unsalted butter, melted and cooled
- Zest of 1 lemon
- 1 tablespoon lemon juice
- A pinch of salt
- Powdered sugar, for dusting (optional)

Instructions:

Preheat Oven:

Preheat your oven to 375°F (190°C). Grease and flour your madeleine molds.

Prepare Lemon Verbena:

Finely chop the fresh lemon verbena leaves.

Beat Eggs and Sugar:

In a mixing bowl, beat the eggs and granulated sugar together until light and fluffy.

Sift Dry Ingredients:

In a separate bowl, sift together the all-purpose flour, baking powder, and a pinch of salt.

Add Dry Ingredients to Egg Mixture:

Gradually fold the sifted dry ingredients into the egg and sugar mixture until well combined.

Add Lemon Verbena, Lemon Zest, and Juice:

Mix in the finely chopped lemon verbena, lemon zest, and lemon juice. Stir until the ingredients are evenly distributed.

Add Melted Butter:

Pour in the melted and cooled unsalted butter and fold it into the batter until smooth.

Chill Batter:

Cover the batter with plastic wrap and let it chill in the refrigerator for at least 1 hour. This step helps the madeleines develop their characteristic hump.

Fill Madeleine Molds:

Spoon the chilled batter into the prepared madeleine molds, filling each mold almost to the top.

Bake:

Bake in the preheated oven for about 10-12 minutes or until the madeleines are golden brown around the edges and have a slight hump in the center.

Cool:

Remove the madeleines from the molds and let them cool on a wire rack.

Dust with Powdered Sugar:

Optionally, dust the Lemon Verbena Madeleines with powdered sugar before serving.

Enjoy these fragrant and citrusy Lemon Verbena Madeleines with a cup of tea or coffee for a delightful treat. The unique flavor of lemon verbena adds a refreshing twist to this classic French pastry.

Strawberry Rhubarb Tart

Ingredients:

For the Tart Crust:

- 1 1/4 cups (160g) all-purpose flour
- 1/4 cup (50g) granulated sugar
- 1/2 cup (1 stick or 113g) unsalted butter, chilled and cut into small pieces
- 1 large egg yolk
- 2 tablespoons ice water

For the Filling:

- 2 cups fresh rhubarb, diced
- 2 cups fresh strawberries, hulled and sliced
- 1/2 cup (100g) granulated sugar
- 1/4 cup (30g) cornstarch
- 1 teaspoon vanilla extract
- Zest of 1 lemon

For the Glaze:

- 1/4 cup strawberry jam or preserves
- 1 tablespoon water

Instructions:

For the Tart Crust:

Prepare Crust Dough:

In a food processor, combine the all-purpose flour and granulated sugar. Add the chilled, diced butter and pulse until the mixture resembles coarse crumbs.

Add Egg Yolk and Water:

Add the egg yolk and ice water to the mixture. Pulse until the dough comes together. If needed, add more water, one tablespoon at a time.

Form Dough:

Turn the dough out onto a floured surface and gently knead it to form a smooth disk. Wrap it in plastic wrap and refrigerate for at least 30 minutes.

Preheat Oven:

Preheat your oven to 375°F (190°C).

Roll Out Dough:

Roll out the chilled dough on a floured surface to fit your tart pan. Press the dough into the pan, ensuring it covers the bottom and sides evenly. Trim any excess dough.

Blind Bake:

Line the tart crust with parchment paper and fill it with pie weights or dried beans. Blind bake for 15 minutes. Remove the weights and parchment, then bake for an additional 5-7 minutes, or until the crust is golden brown. Allow it to cool.

For the Filling:

Prepare Rhubarb and Strawberries:

In a bowl, combine the diced rhubarb and sliced strawberries.

Add Sugar and Cornstarch:

In a separate bowl, mix together granulated sugar and cornstarch. Add this mixture to the rhubarb and strawberries, tossing until the fruit is evenly coated.

Add Vanilla and Lemon Zest:

Stir in the vanilla extract and lemon zest, ensuring all ingredients are well combined.

Fill Tart Shell:

Pour the fruit mixture into the pre-baked tart shell, spreading it out evenly.

For the Glaze:

Make Strawberry Glaze:

In a small saucepan, heat the strawberry jam or preserves with water over low heat until melted and smooth.

Glaze the Tart:

Brush the strawberry glaze over the top of the fruit in the tart.

Chill and Serve:

Chill the Strawberry Rhubarb Tart in the refrigerator for at least 2 hours before serving. Slice and enjoy!

This Strawberry Rhubarb Tart is perfect for spring and summer, showcasing the seasonal flavors of fresh strawberries and rhubarb in a buttery crust. Serve it with a dollop of whipped cream or a scoop of vanilla ice cream for an extra treat.

Gateau Basque

Ingredients:

For the Dough:

- 2 cups (250g) all-purpose flour
- 1 cup (200g) granulated sugar
- 1 cup (225g) unsalted butter, softened
- 3 large egg yolks
- 1 teaspoon baking powder
- 1/4 teaspoon salt
- Zest of 1 lemon

For the Filling:

- 1 1/2 cups (375g) pastry cream or black cherry jam

For the Egg Wash:

- 1 egg yolk
- 1 tablespoon milk

Instructions:

For the Dough:

Prepare Dough:

In a large mixing bowl, cream together the softened butter and sugar until light and fluffy.

Add Egg Yolks and Zest:

Add the egg yolks one at a time, beating well after each addition. Mix in the lemon zest.

Combine Dry Ingredients:

In a separate bowl, whisk together the flour, baking powder, and salt.

Incorporate Dry Ingredients:

> Gradually add the dry ingredients to the butter mixture, mixing until just combined. Be careful not to overmix.

Form Dough:

> Gather the dough into a ball, flatten it into a disk, wrap it in plastic wrap, and refrigerate for at least 1 hour or overnight.

For Assembly:

Preheat Oven:

> Preheat your oven to 350°F (175°C). Grease and flour a 9-inch (23 cm) tart pan with a removable bottom.

Divide Dough:

> Divide the chilled dough into two portions, one slightly larger than the other.

Roll Out Larger Portion:

> Roll out the larger portion to fit the bottom and sides of the tart pan. Press the dough into the pan, ensuring an even layer.

Add Filling:

> Spread the pastry cream or black cherry jam evenly over the dough in the tart pan.

Roll Out Smaller Portion:

> Roll out the smaller portion of dough to fit as a top layer over the filling. You can create a lattice pattern or a solid layer, depending on your preference.

Seal Edges:

> Seal the edges of the dough layers together, ensuring the filling is completely enclosed.

For the Egg Wash:

Prepare Egg Wash:

In a small bowl, whisk together the egg yolk and milk to create an egg wash.

Brush Egg Wash:

Brush the top of the Gâteau Basque with the egg wash for a golden finish.

Bake:

Bake in the preheated oven for 30-40 minutes or until the top is golden brown.

Cool:

Allow the Gâteau Basque to cool in the tart pan for about 10 minutes before transferring it to a wire rack to cool completely.

Serve:

Once cooled, slice and serve the Gâteau Basque. It's delicious on its own or with a dollop of whipped cream.

Enjoy this traditional French dessert with its rich, buttery pastry and delightful filling!

Raspberry Pistachio Financiers

Ingredients:

- 1 cup (225g) unsalted butter
- 1 cup (120g) almond flour
- 1 cup (100g) powdered sugar
- 1/2 cup (60g) all-purpose flour
- 1/4 cup (30g) pistachio flour (ground pistachios)
- 1/4 teaspoon salt
- 6 large egg whites
- 1 teaspoon vanilla extract
- 1/2 cup fresh raspberries
- 2 tablespoons chopped pistachios (for garnish)

Instructions:

Preheat Oven:

Preheat your oven to 375°F (190°C). Grease and flour a financier mold or a mini muffin pan.

Brown Butter:

In a small saucepan, melt the butter over medium heat. Continue cooking until the butter solids turn golden brown, giving the butter a nutty aroma. Be careful not to burn it. Remove from heat and let it cool slightly.

Prepare Dry Ingredients:

In a mixing bowl, whisk together almond flour, powdered sugar, all-purpose flour, pistachio flour, and salt.

Add Egg Whites:

In a separate bowl, lightly whisk the egg whites until frothy. Add the vanilla extract and whisk again.

Combine Wet and Dry Ingredients:

Pour the browned butter into the dry ingredients and mix until well combined. Add the whisked egg whites gradually, stirring until smooth and homogenous.

Fold in Raspberries:

Gently fold in the fresh raspberries into the batter, being careful not to crush them.

Fill Financier Molds:

Spoon the batter into the prepared financier molds or mini muffin cups, filling each about 3/4 full.

Bake:

Bake in the preheated oven for approximately 12-15 minutes or until the edges are golden brown and a toothpick inserted into the center comes out clean.

Cool:

Allow the Raspberry Pistachio Financiers to cool in the mold for a few minutes before transferring them to a wire rack to cool completely.

Garnish:

Once cooled, you can optionally garnish the tops with chopped pistachios for added texture.

Serve:

Serve these delightful Raspberry Pistachio Financiers as a sweet treat with your favorite hot beverage.

Enjoy the combination of almond, pistachio, and raspberry flavors in these tender and elegant little cakes!

Chocolatine (Pain au Chocolat)

Ingredients:

For the Dough:

- 2 1/4 cups (280g) all-purpose flour
- 1/4 cup (30g) sugar
- 1 teaspoon salt
- 1 1/4 cups (285g) unsalted butter, cold
- 1/2 cup (120ml) cold water

For the Chocolate Filling:

- 4 ounces (115g) high-quality dark chocolate, chopped
- 2 tablespoons unsalted butter
- 2 tablespoons powdered sugar
- 1 tablespoon cocoa powder

For Assembly:

- 1 egg (for egg wash)
- Powdered sugar for dusting (optional)

Instructions:

For the Dough:

Prepare Butter Block:

Cut the cold butter into small cubes and place them on a sheet of plastic wrap. Form a 6-inch square with the butter, wrap it tightly, and refrigerate while preparing the dough.

Make Dough:

In a large bowl, combine the all-purpose flour, sugar, and salt. Gradually add cold water, mixing until the dough comes together. Knead the dough briefly on a floured surface, then shape it into a rectangle. Wrap in plastic wrap and refrigerate for 30 minutes.

Roll Out Dough:

On a floured surface, roll out the chilled dough into a larger rectangle, about twice the size of the butter block.

Encase Butter:

Place the chilled butter block in the center of the rolled-out dough. Fold the dough over the butter to encase it completely. Seal the edges.

Perform First Fold (Single Turn):

Roll out the dough to a rectangle and fold it into thirds, like a business letter. This is the first fold. Wrap the dough in plastic wrap and refrigerate for at least 30 minutes.

Perform Additional Folds:

Repeat the rolling and folding process (two more times) for a total of three folds. Rest the dough in the refrigerator for at least 30 minutes between each fold.

Final Rest:

After the last fold, refrigerate the laminated dough for at least 1 hour or overnight.

For the Chocolate Filling:

Prepare Chocolate Filling:

In a heatproof bowl set over a pot of simmering water, melt the chopped dark chocolate and butter, stirring until smooth. Remove from heat and stir in powdered sugar and cocoa powder until well combined. Let it cool.

For Assembly:

Preheat Oven:

Preheat your oven to 400°F (200°C).

Roll Out and Fill Dough:

On a floured surface, roll out the laminated dough into a rectangle. Spread the chocolate filling evenly over the surface.

Fold and Cut:

Fold the dough in half lengthwise, covering the chocolate. Cut the folded dough into equal-sized rectangles.

Place on Baking Sheet:

Place the filled pastries on a parchment-lined baking sheet.

Brush with Egg Wash:

In a small bowl, beat the egg and brush it over the tops of the Chocolatines for a golden finish.

Bake:

Bake in the preheated oven for 15-20 minutes or until the Chocolatines are puffed and golden brown.

Cool and Dust:

Allow the Chocolatines to cool on a wire rack. Optionally, dust with powdered sugar before serving.

Enjoy these homemade Chocolatines with a cup of coffee or tea for a delightful French breakfast or snack!

Pear Frangipane Tart

Ingredients:

For the Tart Crust:

- 1 1/4 cups (160g) all-purpose flour
- 1/2 cup (60g) powdered sugar
- 1/2 cup (1 stick or 113g) unsalted butter, cold and cut into small cubes
- 1 large egg yolk
- 1-2 tablespoons cold water

For the Frangipane Filling:

- 1 cup (100g) almond flour
- 1/2 cup (100g) granulated sugar
- 1/2 cup (1 stick or 113g) unsalted butter, softened
- 2 large eggs
- 1 teaspoon vanilla extract
- 1 tablespoon all-purpose flour

For Assembly:

- 2-3 ripe pears, peeled, cored, and thinly sliced
- Apricot jam or honey for glazing

Instructions:

For the Tart Crust:

Prepare Crust Dough:

In a food processor, combine the all-purpose flour and powdered sugar. Add the cold, cubed butter, and pulse until the mixture resembles coarse crumbs.

Add Egg Yolk and Water:

Add the egg yolk and 1 tablespoon of cold water. Pulse until the dough comes together. If needed, add an additional tablespoon of water.

Form Dough:

Turn the dough out onto a floured surface and gather it into a ball. Flatten it into a disk, wrap it in plastic wrap, and refrigerate for at least 30 minutes.

Preheat Oven:

Preheat your oven to 375°F (190°C).

Roll Out Dough:

Roll out the chilled dough on a floured surface to fit a tart pan. Press the dough into the tart pan, ensuring an even layer. Trim any excess dough.

Blind Bake:

Line the tart crust with parchment paper and fill it with pie weights or dried beans. Blind bake for 15 minutes. Remove the weights and parchment, then bake for an additional 5-7 minutes, or until the crust is golden brown. Allow it to cool.

For the Frangipane Filling:

Prepare Frangipane Filling:

In a bowl, beat together almond flour, granulated sugar, softened butter, eggs, vanilla extract, and 1 tablespoon of all-purpose flour until smooth and well combined.

For Assembly:

Spread Frangipane in Crust:

Spread the frangipane filling evenly over the cooled tart crust.

Arrange Pear Slices:

Arrange the thinly sliced pears over the frangipane filling in an attractive pattern.

Bake:

Bake the Pear Frangipane Tart in the preheated oven for 30-35 minutes or until the frangipane is set and golden brown.

Glaze with Apricot Jam or Honey:

While the tart is still warm, heat apricot jam or honey and brush it over the top of the pears for a shiny glaze.

Cool and Serve:

Allow the Pear Frangipane Tart to cool before slicing. Serve at room temperature and enjoy!

This Pear Frangipane Tart is a perfect combination of buttery crust, almond filling, and the sweetness of ripe pears. It's a lovely dessert for any occasion.

Tiramisu Eclairs

Ingredients:

For the Éclair Pastry:

- 1/2 cup (1 stick or 113g) unsalted butter
- 1 cup water
- 1 cup all-purpose flour
- 1/4 teaspoon salt
- 4 large eggs

For the Mascarpone Filling:

- 1 cup (240ml) heavy cream
- 1 cup (250g) mascarpone cheese, softened
- 1/2 cup (60g) powdered sugar
- 1 teaspoon vanilla extract

For the Coffee Soaking Syrup:

- 1/2 cup strong brewed coffee, cooled
- 2 tablespoons coffee liqueur (optional)
- 2 tablespoons sugar

For the Tiramisu Topping:

- Cocoa powder for dusting

Instructions:

For the Éclair Pastry:

Preheat Oven:

Preheat your oven to 400°F (200°C). Line a baking sheet with parchment paper.

Make Choux Pastry:

In a saucepan, combine butter, water, and salt. Bring to a boil. Remove from heat and quickly stir in the flour until well combined. Return to low heat and continue stirring for a minute or two until the mixture forms a smooth ball.

Add Eggs:

Allow the mixture to cool for a few minutes, then add the eggs one at a time, beating well after each addition. The dough should be smooth and glossy.

Pipe Éclairs:

Transfer the choux pastry dough to a piping bag fitted with a large round tip. Pipe 4-5 inch (10-12 cm) long éclairs onto the prepared baking sheet, leaving space between each.

Bake:

Bake in the preheated oven for 15-20 minutes or until the éclairs are puffed and golden brown. Reduce the oven temperature to 350°F (180°C) and continue baking for an additional 10 minutes to ensure the centers are cooked through. Allow the éclairs to cool completely.

For the Mascarpone Filling:

Whip Cream:

In a bowl, whip the heavy cream until stiff peaks form.

Make Mascarpone Mixture:

In another bowl, combine the softened mascarpone cheese, powdered sugar, and vanilla extract. Gently fold in the whipped cream until smooth.

For the Coffee Soaking Syrup:

Prepare Coffee Syrup:

In a bowl, mix together the cooled strong brewed coffee, coffee liqueur (if using), and sugar until the sugar dissolves.

Assembly:

Cut and Fill Éclairs:

> Cut the cooled éclairs in half horizontally. Dip the top halves into the coffee soaking syrup.

Fill with Mascarpone Cream:

> Pipe or spoon the mascarpone filling onto the bottom halves of the éclairs. Place the soaked tops on the filled bottoms.

Dust with Cocoa:

> Dust the Tiramisu Éclairs with cocoa powder.

Chill:

> Chill the filled éclairs in the refrigerator for at least 1-2 hours before serving.

Serve these Tiramisu Éclairs chilled for a delightful fusion of French and Italian flavors in a single, elegant pastry!

Apricot Pistachio Galette

Ingredients:

For the Galette Dough:

- 1 1/4 cups (160g) all-purpose flour
- 1 tablespoon granulated sugar
- 1/4 teaspoon salt
- 1/2 cup (1 stick or 113g) unsalted butter, cold and cut into small cubes
- 3-4 tablespoons ice water

For the Apricot Pistachio Filling:

- 4 cups fresh apricots, pitted and sliced
- 1/3 cup granulated sugar
- 2 tablespoons cornstarch
- 1 teaspoon vanilla extract

For Assembly:

- 1/2 cup (60g) chopped pistachios
- 1 tablespoon apricot jam (for glazing)
- Powdered sugar for dusting (optional)
- Vanilla ice cream or whipped cream (optional, for serving)

Instructions:

For the Galette Dough:

Prepare Dough:

In a food processor, combine the all-purpose flour, granulated sugar, and salt. Add the cold, cubed butter and pulse until the mixture resembles coarse crumbs.

Add Ice Water:

With the processor running, gradually add ice water, one tablespoon at a time, until the dough just comes together.

Form Dough:

Turn the dough out onto a floured surface and gather it into a ball. Flatten it into a disk, wrap it in plastic wrap, and refrigerate for at least 30 minutes.

For the Apricot Pistachio Filling:

Prepare Filling:

In a bowl, toss together the sliced apricots, granulated sugar, cornstarch, and vanilla extract until well combined. Let the mixture sit for about 10 minutes.

For Assembly:

Preheat Oven:

Preheat your oven to 375°F (190°C). Line a baking sheet with parchment paper.

Roll Out Dough:

On a floured surface, roll out the chilled galette dough into a circle about 12 inches in diameter.

Transfer Dough:

Carefully transfer the rolled-out dough to the prepared baking sheet.

Arrange Apricot Filling:

Arrange the apricot filling in the center of the dough, leaving a border around the edges.

Fold and Seal:

Fold the edges of the dough over the apricot filling, pleating as needed. Press the edges to seal.

Brush with Apricot Jam:

In a small saucepan, heat the apricot jam until melted. Brush the melted jam over the apricots for a glossy finish.

Sprinkle with Pistachios:

> Sprinkle the chopped pistachios over the apricot filling.

Bake:

> Bake in the preheated oven for 35-40 minutes or until the crust is golden brown and the apricots are tender.

Cool:

> Allow the Apricot Pistachio Galette to cool on the baking sheet for a few minutes before transferring it to a wire rack to cool completely.

Dust with Powdered Sugar:

> Optionally, dust the galette with powdered sugar before serving.

Serve:

> Serve slices of the galette on their own or with a scoop of vanilla ice cream or a dollop of whipped cream if desired.

This Apricot Pistachio Galette is a delightful summer dessert, perfect for showcasing the flavors of ripe apricots and the crunch of pistachios in a simple and beautiful rustic tart.

Matcha Green Tea Madeleines

Ingredients:

- 2 tablespoons matcha green tea powder
- 2/3 cup (130g) granulated sugar
- 3 large eggs, at room temperature
- 1 cup (125g) all-purpose flour
- 1 teaspoon baking powder
- 1/2 cup (1 stick or 113g) unsalted butter, melted and cooled
- 1 teaspoon vanilla extract
- Powdered sugar (for dusting, optional)

Instructions:

Preheat Oven:

Preheat your oven to 350°F (180°C). Grease and flour your madeleine molds.

Sift Matcha Powder:

Sift the matcha green tea powder to ensure there are no lumps.

Combine Matcha and Sugar:

In a bowl, whisk together the sifted matcha powder and granulated sugar.

Beat Eggs:

In a separate bowl, beat the eggs until they are light and fluffy.

Add Matcha Sugar Mixture:

Gradually add the matcha sugar mixture to the beaten eggs, whisking continuously until well combined.

Sift Flour and Baking Powder:

In another bowl, sift together the all-purpose flour and baking powder.

Fold in Dry Ingredients:

Gently fold the sifted flour and baking powder into the matcha and egg mixture until just combined.

Add Melted Butter and Vanilla:

Pour in the melted and cooled unsalted butter and add the vanilla extract. Fold until the batter is smooth.

Chill Batter:

Cover the batter with plastic wrap and refrigerate for at least 1 hour or overnight. This step helps the madeleines develop their characteristic hump.

Preheat Oven Again:

Preheat your oven to 375°F (190°C).

Fill Madeleine Molds:

Spoon the chilled batter into the prepared madeleine molds, filling each mold almost to the top.

Bake:

Bake in the preheated oven for about 10-12 minutes or until the madeleines are set and have a slight hump in the center.

Cool:

Remove the madeleines from the molds and let them cool on a wire rack.

Dust with Powdered Sugar:

Optionally, dust the Matcha Green Tea Madeleines with powdered sugar before serving.

These Matcha Green Tea Madeleines are a delightful treat with a subtle and earthy flavor from the matcha powder. Enjoy them with a cup of tea or coffee for a lovely and elegant dessert experience.

Peach Melba Millefeuille

Ingredients:

For the Puff Pastry:

- 1 sheet of puff pastry, thawed if frozen

For the Vanilla Pastry Cream:

- 2 cups (480ml) whole milk
- 1/2 cup (100g) granulated sugar
- 4 large egg yolks
- 1/4 cup (30g) cornstarch
- 1 teaspoon vanilla extract
- 2 tablespoons unsalted butter

For Assembly:

- 2-3 ripe peaches, peeled and thinly sliced
- 1 cup fresh raspberries
- 2 tablespoons powdered sugar (for dusting)

Instructions:

For the Puff Pastry:

Preheat Oven:

Preheat your oven according to the puff pastry package instructions.

Roll and Cut Puff Pastry:

Roll out the puff pastry on a lightly floured surface. Cut it into rectangular pieces of equal size. Place the pieces on a baking sheet lined with parchment paper.

Bake:

Bake the puff pastry according to the package instructions or until it is golden brown and puffed. Allow it to cool completely.

For the Vanilla Pastry Cream:

Prepare Vanilla Pastry Cream:

    In a saucepan, heat the whole milk until it just starts to simmer.

Whisk Egg Yolks and Sugar:

    In a separate bowl, whisk together the egg yolks and sugar until pale and well combined.

Add Cornstarch:

    Add the cornstarch to the egg yolk mixture and whisk until smooth.

Temper Egg Yolks:

    Gradually pour the hot milk into the egg yolk mixture, whisking constantly. This tempers the eggs and prevents them from curdling.

Cook and Thicken:

    Return the mixture to the saucepan and cook over medium heat, stirring constantly, until it thickens into a custard-like consistency. This should take a few minutes.

Add Vanilla and Butter:

    Remove the saucepan from heat and stir in the vanilla extract and butter until smooth. Allow the pastry cream to cool.

For Assembly:

Assemble Millefeuille:

    Assemble the Peach Melba Millefeuille by layering the cooled puff pastry with the vanilla pastry cream, sliced peaches, and fresh raspberries. Repeat the layers as desired.

Top with Raspberry Sauce:

    Drizzle the top layer with raspberry sauce.

Dust with Powdered Sugar:

    Dust the assembled Peach Melba Millefeuille with powdered sugar.

Chill:

> Refrigerate the assembled dessert for at least 1-2 hours to allow the flavors to meld and the pastry cream to set.

Serve:

> Slice and serve the Peach Melba Millefeuille, enjoying the combination of flaky pastry, creamy vanilla, and the freshness of peaches and raspberries.

This Peach Melba Millefeuille is a visually stunning and delicious dessert, perfect for summer occasions. The layers of puff pastry, vanilla pastry cream, and fresh fruits create a delightful balance of textures and flavors.

Blueberry Lavender Macarons

Ingredients:

For the Macaron Shells:

- 1 cup (100g) almond flour
- 1 3/4 cups (210g) powdered sugar
- 3 large egg whites, at room temperature
- 1/4 cup (50g) granulated sugar
- Blue gel food coloring

For the Blueberry Lavender Ganache:

- 1/2 cup fresh or frozen blueberries
- 1 tablespoon dried culinary lavender
- 1/2 cup (120ml) heavy cream
- 8 ounces (225g) white chocolate, finely chopped
- 2 tablespoons unsalted butter, softened

Instructions:

For the Macaron Shells:

Prepare Baking Sheets:

Line two baking sheets with parchment paper.

Process Almond Flour and Powdered Sugar:

In a food processor, combine almond flour and powdered sugar. Process until finely ground. Sift the mixture to ensure a smooth texture.

Whip Egg Whites:

In a clean, dry bowl, beat the egg whites until foamy. Gradually add granulated sugar, continuing to beat until glossy stiff peaks form. Add a few drops of blue gel food coloring and continue to beat until the color is evenly distributed.

Fold in Dry Ingredients:

Gently fold the sifted almond flour and powdered sugar mixture into the whipped egg whites until well combined. Be careful not to deflate the batter.

Pipe Macarons:

Transfer the batter to a piping bag fitted with a round tip. Pipe small rounds onto the prepared baking sheets. Let the piped macarons rest for about 30 minutes to an hour until a skin forms on the surface.

Preheat Oven:

Preheat your oven to 300°F (150°C).

Bake:

Bake the macarons in the preheated oven for 15-18 minutes or until the shells are set and have smooth, shiny tops. Allow them to cool completely before removing from the parchment paper.

For the Blueberry Lavender Ganache:

Prepare Blueberry Lavender Infusion:

In a small saucepan, combine the blueberries, dried lavender, and heavy cream. Heat the mixture over medium heat until it simmers. Remove from heat and let it steep for about 15 minutes.

Strain and Reheat:

Strain the blueberry lavender mixture to remove solids. Reheat the infused cream until it's hot but not boiling.

Pour Over White Chocolate:

Place the finely chopped white chocolate in a heatproof bowl. Pour the hot infused cream over the chocolate and let it sit for a minute. Stir until the chocolate is melted and smooth.

Add Butter:

Add the softened butter to the ganache and mix until well combined. Let the ganache cool and thicken.

Assemble Macarons:

Match the macaron shells into pairs of similar sizes. Pipe or spoon a small amount of the blueberry lavender ganache onto one shell and sandwich it with another.

Chill:

Place the filled macarons in an airtight container and refrigerate for at least 24 hours to allow the flavors to meld and the texture to develop.

Serve:

Bring the Blueberry Lavender Macarons to room temperature before serving.

These Blueberry Lavender Macarons offer a delightful blend of floral and fruity flavors, making them a unique and sophisticated treat. Enjoy these elegant macarons with a cup of tea or as a special dessert for any occasion.

Orange Blossom Madeleine Tartlets

Ingredients:

For the Madeleine Tartlets:

- 1 cup (2 sticks or 226g) unsalted butter, melted and cooled
- 4 large eggs
- 1 cup (200g) granulated sugar
- 2 cups (250g) all-purpose flour
- 1 teaspoon baking powder
- Pinch of salt
- 1 tablespoon orange blossom water
- Zest of 2 oranges

For the Orange Blossom Glaze:

- 1 cup (120g) powdered sugar
- 2-3 tablespoons orange blossom water
- Orange zest for garnish (optional)

Instructions:

For the Madeleine Tartlets:

Preheat Oven:

Preheat your oven to 350°F (180°C). Grease and flour mini tartlet pans.

Prepare Madeleine Batter:

In a large mixing bowl, whisk together the melted butter, eggs, and granulated sugar until well combined.

Combine Dry Ingredients:

In a separate bowl, sift together the all-purpose flour, baking powder, and a pinch of salt.

Incorporate Dry Ingredients:

Gradually add the dry ingredients to the wet ingredients, mixing until just combined. Be careful not to overmix.

Add Orange Blossom Water and Zest:

Stir in the orange blossom water and the zest of 2 oranges. Mix until the batter is smooth and well incorporated.

Fill Tartlet Pans:

Spoon the madeleine batter into the prepared mini tartlet pans, filling each cavity about 3/4 full.

Bake:

Bake in the preheated oven for 12-15 minutes or until the madeleines are golden brown and spring back when touched.

Cool:

Allow the madeleine tartlets to cool in the pans for a few minutes before transferring them to a wire rack to cool completely.

For the Orange Blossom Glaze:

Prepare Glaze:

In a bowl, whisk together the powdered sugar and orange blossom water until you achieve a smooth glaze.

Glaze Tartlets:

Once the madeleine tartlets are completely cooled, drizzle the orange blossom glaze over the tops of the tartlets.

Garnish (Optional):

Optionally, garnish the glazed tartlets with additional orange zest for a burst of citrus aroma.

Serve:

> Allow the glaze to set before serving. Once set, serve these delightful Orange Blossom Madeleine Tartlets and enjoy the delicate citrus and floral flavors.

These Orange Blossom Madeleine Tartlets are perfect for a tea-time treat or as a sweet ending to a special meal. The combination of orange blossom water and orange zest adds a refreshing and aromatic twist to the classic madeleine.

Hazelnut Dacquoise

Ingredients:

For the Hazelnut Meringue Layers:

- 1 cup (120g) hazelnuts, toasted and finely ground
- 1 cup (120g) confectioners' sugar
- 4 large egg whites, at room temperature
- 1/2 cup (100g) granulated sugar
- 1 teaspoon vanilla extract

For the Hazelnut Praline Buttercream Filling:

- 1/2 cup (120g) hazelnut praline paste
- 1 cup (2 sticks or 226g) unsalted butter, softened
- 1 cup (120g) confectioners' sugar
- 1 teaspoon vanilla extract

Instructions:

For the Hazelnut Meringue Layers:

Preheat Oven:

Preheat your oven to 300°F (150°C). Line two baking sheets with parchment paper.

Prepare Hazelnuts:

Toast the hazelnuts in the oven until they become fragrant, about 10 minutes. Allow them to cool, then finely grind them in a food processor with the confectioners' sugar.

Whip Egg Whites:

In a clean, dry bowl, whip the egg whites until soft peaks form. Gradually add the granulated sugar while continuing to whip. Beat until glossy stiff peaks form.

Fold in Hazelnut Mixture:

Gently fold the ground hazelnuts and confectioners' sugar mixture into the whipped egg whites. Add vanilla extract and continue folding until just combined.

Pipe Meringue Layers:

Transfer the hazelnut meringue mixture to a piping bag fitted with a round tip. Pipe circles or rectangles onto the prepared baking sheets.

Bake:

Bake in the preheated oven for about 25-30 minutes or until the meringue layers are firm and slightly golden. Allow them to cool completely.

For the Hazelnut Praline Buttercream Filling:

Prepare Hazelnut Praline Paste:

If you don't have hazelnut praline paste, you can make it by blending toasted hazelnuts and sugar in a food processor until smooth.

Make Hazelnut Praline Buttercream:

In a bowl, beat together the hazelnut praline paste, softened butter, confectioners' sugar, and vanilla extract until creamy and well combined.

Assembly:

Assemble Hazelnut Dacquoise:

Place one layer of hazelnut meringue on a serving plate. Spread a layer of hazelnut praline buttercream on top. Repeat the process with additional layers until you reach the desired height.

Chill:

Chill the Hazelnut Dacquoise in the refrigerator for at least 2 hours to allow the flavors to meld and the buttercream to set.

Serve:

Slice and serve the Hazelnut Dacquoise. Optionally, you can garnish with chopped hazelnuts or a dusting of confectioners' sugar.

Enjoy this Hazelnut Dacquoise as a rich and nutty dessert with a combination of crunchy meringue and creamy hazelnut praline buttercream. It's a perfect treat for special occasions.

Prune Armagnac Clafoutis

Ingredients:

- 1 cup pitted prunes
- 1/2 cup Armagnac (or brandy)
- 3 large eggs
- 1/2 cup granulated sugar
- 1 cup whole milk
- 1/2 cup heavy cream
- 1 teaspoon vanilla extract
- 1/2 cup all-purpose flour
- Pinch of salt
- Powdered sugar for dusting

Instructions:

Soak Prunes in Armagnac:

Place the pitted prunes in a bowl and pour the Armagnac over them. Allow them to soak for at least 1-2 hours or overnight, allowing the prunes to absorb the flavors.

Preheat Oven:

Preheat your oven to 350°F (180°C). Grease a baking dish or individual ramekins.

Prepare Batter:

In a blender, combine eggs, granulated sugar, milk, heavy cream, vanilla extract, flour, and a pinch of salt. Blend until the batter is smooth and well combined.

Drain and Arrange Prunes:

Drain the soaked prunes and arrange them in the greased baking dish or ramekins.

Pour Batter Over Prunes:

Pour the batter over the prunes in the baking dish, ensuring that they are evenly covered.

Bake:

Bake in the preheated oven for about 40-45 minutes or until the clafoutis is set and golden brown on top. It may puff up during baking but will deflate slightly as it cools.

Cool:

Allow the Prune Armagnac Clafoutis to cool for a bit before serving. It can be served warm or at room temperature.

Dust with Powdered Sugar:

Dust the top of the clafoutis with powdered sugar just before serving.

Serve:

Serve slices of the Prune Armagnac Clafoutis as a delicious and boozy dessert.

This Prune Armagnac Clafoutis is a wonderful combination of rich custard, soaked prunes, and the warmth of Armagnac. It makes for a sophisticated and comforting dessert, perfect for special occasions or a cozy evening treat.

www.ingramcontent.com/pod-product-compliance
Lightning Source LLC
LaVergne TN
LVHW061936070526
838199LV00060B/3849